WRITING MYSTERIES FOR YOUNG PEOPLE

BOOKS BY JOAN LOWERY NIXON

Books for Young People

THE MYSTERY OF HURRICANE CASTLE
THE MYSTERY OF THE GRINNING IDOL
THE MYSTERY OF THE HIDDEN COCKATOO
THE MYSTERY OF THE HAUNTED WOODS
THE MYSTERY OF THE SECRET STOWAWAY
DELBERT, THE PLAINCLOTHES DETECTIVE
THE ALLIGATOR UNDER THE BED
THE SECRET BOX MYSTERY
THE MYSTERIOUS RED TAPE GANG
THE MYSTERIOUS PROWLER
WHO IS MY NEIGHBOR?
FIVE LOAVES AND TWO FISHES
THE SON WHO CAME HOME AGAIN
OIL AND GAS, FROM FOSSILS TO FUELS (CO-AUTHOR)

Books for Adults

GOD AND GRANDMOTHERS

Textbooks

PEOPLE AND ME (CO-AUTHOR)
THIS I CAN BE (CO-AUTHOR)
WRITING MYSTERIES FOR YOUNG PEOPLE

WRITING MYSTERIES
FOR
YOUNG PEOPLE

by
Joan Lowery Nixon

Publishers   **THE WRITER, INC.**   *Boston*

Copyright © 1977 by Joan Lowery Nixon

Library of Congress Cataloging in Publication Data

Nixon, Joan Lowery.
    Writing mysteries for young people.

    1. Children's stories — Authorship. 2. Detective and
mystery stories — Authorship. I. Title.
PN3377.N59   808.3'872   77-5337
ISBN 0-87116-108-7

Printed in the United States of America

Contents

v

Acknowledgments

With thanks to those who have always been there with help
and encouragement:
  my parents,
  my children,
  my writer and editor friends,
  and in particular to the most important one of all —
  my husband, Nick.

Introduction

At that wonderful period in life—between the ages of eight and twelve—children have improved in their reading skills to the point at which they are able to read on their own. They explore everything: fantasy, biography, science, adventure, humor; but a perennial favorite is the mystery.

They are old enough to be brave, and being brave, they like to be scared. They want to move outward into adventure. If they can't do this physically, they can at least relate enthusiastically to the heroes and heroines of mystery novels, who courageously take on threatening, frightening situations and win.

Since mystery stories are now found in picture books and easy-to-read books for beginning readers, and the mystery novel is a staple on any list for young adult readers, writing in these categories will be discussed in later chapters of this book. But the main emphasis will be on writing the mystery novel for readers eight to twelve.

The techniques that result in a good mystery story or novel also can be applied to writing a good general story or longer work of fiction, but how these techniques relate to the mystery will be the major focus of this book.

The craft of writing for children can be learned: how to give depth to the main character; how to write dialogue and how and when to use it in place of narration; how to build effective, convincing plots, and how to make good use of subplots; how to begin a story and where to end it; how to chart a novel, step by step; and how to use plants, clues, and red herrings. These points are just a few of the many approaches and techniques that will be discussed for the aspiring writer of mysteries for young people.

Mystery novels include a wide variety of types: the straight modern mystery, the occult, the historical tale, and the adventure yarn of today or long ago. The plots fall into two categories—the traditional mystery and the suspense novel.

The suspense novel is, of course, also a mystery novel, although the forms differ. In the mystery, the readers and the hero or heroine do not know who the villain is until the end of the story. In the suspense novel, the crime and the criminal may be known at or near the beginning of the story, or in the course of the story, with readers aware of every frightening detail. Readers are made to wonder how the villain will be caught and if the protagonist in the story will escape from harm; they will follow the chase or the process of detection with growing suspense—and breathe a sigh of relief at the end.

The juvenile mystery can combine the best writing in children's literature with a plot so exciting that young readers cannot put it down. Some people continue to believe that all juvenile mysteries must have stock characters in stereotyped situations (remembering from childhood, no doubt, the pattern of some series mysteries) and therefore think that mysteries should not be seriously considered as anything more than light entertainment. But a larger—and growing—number view the juvenile mystery as quality writing that provides new horizons and new directions of thought for young readers. For this reason, more and more juvenile mysteries are published, reviewed, appear on recommended book lists, and are avidly read by countless numbers of children. And it is for these reasons that writers like you and me can find so much satisfaction in writing mysteries for young people.

J.L.N.

WRITING MYSTERIES FOR YOUNG PEOPLE

1

Getting the Idea: First Steps

THE QUESTION, "Where do you get your ideas?" is probably the one most often asked of writers, and it's one that can be easily answered. Ideas come from many directions. It's up to a writer to keep on the watch for them, to grab them before they dash past. As looking for ideas becomes a habit, more ideas will turn up than a writer can handle.

Most writers keep notebooks in which to record ideas—scraps of dialogue, a factual newspaper clipping that sparks an idea, a sudden thought that occurs and could be developed later. I jot down many of my ideas on small sheets of paper and transfer them to a large bulletin board in my office. At the moment, these slips of paper and short clippings include a section of a letter from my mother telling about a mysterious thing that happened to her and my father when their car broke down in a quiet neighborhood; a political column on the problems of Interpol (the International Criminal Police Organization); a newspaper interview with a man who is a ghost-hunter; and three slips of paper with mystery novel ideas which occurred to me. Some of these ideas might eventually find their way into juvenile mystery novels.

Idea sources

There is rarely an explanation in a mystery novel in which the author traces the source and development of the idea; but in *Pageants of Despair,* Dennis Hamley tells how he came to write the book, which takes the hero back to the fifteenth century and to the miracle plays that were produced in the villages of England at that time. He writes that he found a description of an incident that took place at the end of the sixteenth century, when Marlowe's *Faust,* a play about a man who sold his soul to the devil, was being performed. An extra devil suddenly appeared on stage, and the audience and actors ran away in terror and panic, sure that the extra devil was no mortal actor. This legend and Hamley's interest in the old morality plays were the springboards to the idea he later developed into that juvenile mystery novel.

Newspaper or magazine articles are often good sources for mystery ideas. A newspaper feature story about a change in values among the young people in a Southwest Indian tribe eventually led to my book, *The Mystery of the Haunted Woods.* According to the article, many young people wanted to leave the reservation and go away to college, while the older people wanted them to stay so the tribe could remain a unit. I was familiar with a number of abandoned Western mining towns that were now simply collections of deteriorating buildings—ideal ghost towns. And I had worked with a woman in our town who was passionately eager to learn, and who studied at every opportunity. Here was my springboard—pieces that could be fitted together to make a unit of character and plot.

I located the abandoned town in the mountains of New Mexico; and the woman I knew became an Indian girl, Lily, who wanted desperately to continue her education by going to college, against the stern disapproval of her grandmother, who wanted only to see her grandchild married and settled as a housewife in the tribe.

My main characters in the story—two young sisters, who had appeared in one of my earlier books—are mystified and frightened by some strange happenings, and especially by their discovery that the "ghost town" in the woods on their aunt's vast ranch property seems to be inhabited by a ghost who tries to frighten them away. At the climax of the book, they discover the "ghost" is Lily, who has made a study area for herself in one of the old buildings and is secretly being tutored by a sympathetic teacher from town. The children, with the help of their aunt, work out a solution to the problem that Lily's grandmother can accept.

Items in the news should never be treated exactly as they happened but should be turned into original, unusual plots. About a year after a national news story came out about people stealing trees from each other (as certain types of wood became more valuable), an editor speaking at a writers' conference said, "It's the strangest coincidence. In the space of one week, I've received three juvenile novels from authors in different parts of the country on the same topic—the theft of trees!" Just remember that other writers are out there looking for ideas, too!

A personal experience can readily grow into a complete idea for a book-length mystery. At the end of our first year in Texas, we found ourselves in the middle of Hurricane Carla. Although the city in which we lived, Corpus Christi, suffered relatively minor damage when the eye of the hurricane shifted north, we saw the total destruction of some of the beach areas. I wondered what it would be like to be trapped in a hurricane of such force, to have missed being evacuated with the others by some strange set of circumstances, and to try to find safety. I began thinking about characters to go with this problem. They would have to be

children in the eight-to-twelve category, of course; and I
would certainly have to provide them with a means to save
their lives. I created a sturdy, stone, castle-like house at the
top of a cliff; and then, to make the problem more complex, I installed a ghost in the castle and added a local
superstition so that no one in the town would dare to go
near this frightening edifice. What would happen when the
children had to enter the castle in order to remain alive?
How would they deal with this ghost? My answers grew into
The Mystery of Hurricane Castle.

Ghosts, spirits, and devils

Children love scary buildings—castles or others—in their
mystery fiction. They enjoy reading about ghosts and secret
panels and hidden treasure and . . . but wait. These have
been written about countless times. How can writers use
these traditional mystery ideas again?

Authors can take the old favorites and give them a new
touch, using imagination to add something excitingly different. The ghost in *The Mystery of Hurricane Castle* turned
out to be a woman—a recluse hiding from society because of
a facial disfigurement, a kind person who needed acceptance
and understanding.

But ghosts can be unexplained, disembodied spirits who
grow from an idea in the author's imagination into characters in juvenile mysteries. Among the ghosts in current
fiction we find a tried-and-true, standard English ghost who
adds a touch of comedy to the proceedings; a sad young
woman who cannot rest until the true story of her death by
drowning is uncovered; and a few horrifying specters
straight from the dark unknown.

While there was a time in which ghosts were ultimately
explained as really not being ghosts, so that children
wouldn't be frightened, there has been a change. Many current mystery novels deal with the occult, with no rational

explanation of the ghosts, spirits or witches involved. Authors can research occult happenings and, with few restrictions, use them as springboards to developing preternatural situations in their juvenile novels.

Scott Corbett's book, *Here Lies the Body,* is an example. Set primarily in a graveyard, the book leads up to a terrifying climax involving a warlock and all the evil powers he can muster. Ann Turnbull's *The Frightened Forest* deals with the release of a witch-like power that possesses the entire countryside, until it meets head-on a stronger occult force that subdues it. It would be impossible, with either of these stories, to find a convincing rationale for the mysterious happenings. Both of these stories are meant to be frightening, and part of the fear they engender comes from the implication that the embodiment of evil is definitely not of this world.

An idea may include not only the mystery itself, but another fiction form. *The White Jade Fox,* by Andre Norton, combines the mystery with science fiction. An orphaned girl, sent to live at an isolated manor home, discovers a mystery hidden at the manor. She becomes involved with an Oriental woman who can change into a white fox and who has as devoted followers the beautiful wild foxes who roam the protected lands surrounding the manor.

A mystery idea can also serve as an idea for an historical novel. *The Mystery Waters of Tonbridge Wells,* by Teri Martini, involves the disappearance of men in Kent, England, at the time when Napoleon reigned in France, and smuggling was rampant along the coast of England. It seems likely that Teri Martini's interest in history led her to the idea that became the springboard for the mystery novel she created.

The spy-adventure-mystery novel is popular with young people. We think of spies as living in a world of their own, but Mabel Esther Allan moved her spy into a familiar family circle, and thereby into a new, original dimension, when one of the teen-aged girls in her novel, *The Formidable Enemy,* discovers that the aunt she is visiting is a secret agent for Great Britain. The countryside of Scotland is an important part of the story, when the two heroines are kidnapped and taken to a house on an island in a remote loch, and must plan their escape.

Setting is often the source of a mystery idea, as it was for my *The Mystery of the Secret Stowaway.* I thought of a luxury liner as the setting for a juvenile mystery—a liner out at sea with an unwilling stowaway aboard. The plot developed from this point, as I imagined what my stowaway would look like and how he would react to his predicament—with the extra problem of having a mystery on board in which he would become involved.

The occupation of the main character or of a principal character can turn an idea into a plot and add a learning situation. In Arnold Madison's *The Secret of the Carved Whale Bone,* the main character, his cousin, and friends try to save his uncle's failing fishing boat business. The treasure hidden somewhere in the house by a relative who lived there long ago is needed by the uncle to provide funds to help him get through a bad tourist season. The problems are compounded by the presence of a newcomer to the island who wants the uncle to fail so he can buy the property. As the boys try to find the treasure, they also help the uncle by working for him. From this situation and these activities the readers learn a great deal about the workings of a fishing-boat-for-hire business.

Most ideas for juvenile mysteries come from situations or events, but sometimes the ideas can grow from an interesting character. For example, in *Delbert, the Plainclothes Detective,* I began with the idea of a young boy who thinks of himself as a real detective helping the police. By trying to keep his eyes and ears open, carefully noticing what is going on around him, he is able to solve a neighborhood crime. Delbert had to have a reason for being a "detective," so I had him encounter a man near the scene of a burglary. The man tells Delbert that he is a plainclothes detective and that Delbert can be one, too. Delbert starts off on the wrong foot by suspecting the school bully, but by working hard at being aware of the things he sees and hears, Delbert discovers who the real burglar is and at the same time helps solve the problems that grow from his own family's interpersonal relationships.

The personal problem runs through every good mystery novel for children, and authors must develop this idea in tandem with the mystery idea. The solution to this personal problem gives the story depth and rounds out the main character so that he or she is not a flat, one-dimensional person. The personal problem should be tied in closely with the main character and be connected with the mystery, so that by the end of the story the solutions to the mystery and to the personal problem are achieved.

In *Secret of Haunted Mesa,* by Phyllis A. Whitney, the main character's personal problem stems from her having an older sister, a beautiful, musically talented girl, who is already a celebrity. Near the beginning of the story, Jenny thinks:

> It wasn't because she was dumb that she couldn't do her schoolwork. She wasn't failing because she was stupid. It was just that she was no longer interested. She had stopped caring and that was a terrible feeling. But she was tired of teachers who said, "Oh, you're Carol Hanford's sister, aren't you? I remember her in eighth grade. She was so bright and pretty. We all loved her."
>
> Okay, Jenny thought. *She* didn't have to be loved. *She* didn't want all that attention Carol thrived on. Or did she? . . .

By the end of the story, along with solving the mystery

which emerges, Jenny learns to appreciate herself and her own talents.

In my novel, *The Mystery of the Hidden Cockatoo,* the main character, Pam, had the problem of being older sister in a large family. She was troubled by never having any privacy and by always having younger children in the way. While visiting her aunt, Pam meets a girl her age who is an only child of artistic, nonconformist parents—a girl who is used to living in an adult world. As they solve the mystery that threatens them both, the two girls learn to accept and enjoy the best of their own family situations.

In *The View from the Cherry Tree,* by Willo Davis Roberts, Rob's problem concerns the fact that no one will pay attention to him. The interest of the entire family is centered on his sister, who is getting married. Even when he tries to tell them that he has witnessed a murder, everyone is too busy to listen to him. He escapes death at the hands of the murderer—who is the only one who has listened to Rob—and his personal problem is solved when he finally makes the members of the family realize that he needs their attention, too.

Letting ideas develop

An idea needs time to grow. It's almost impossible for authors to answer the question, "How long does it take to write a book?" They can give an approximate answer from the time they sit down to their typewriters to the time they put their polished manuscripts into the mail; but they can't estimate all the weeks, months—sometimes even years—that it takes for a story idea to grow and develop into a full-blown, usable plot for a mystery novel. I am a writer who turns new ideas over and over in my mind, analyzing them, adding to them, subtracting from them, going off on new tangents with them at every available quiet moment.

I usually take notes as the idea forms, since I don't want to take the chance of losing what might be an important point. It helps me to think about the idea before I go to sleep, letting my subconscious mind do some of the work during the night.

Finally, the idea begins to take shape. It's strong. It's exciting. It's developing into a plot. Now I'm ready for the next step. . . .

2

Charting the Book

ONCE the idea for a juvenile mystery novel has reached a certain stage in my mind, the book begins to take shape.

Bit by bit, the main character begins to come to life as I think about him (or her), creating a background for him, a family, interests, likes and dislikes. I might imagine him in various situations. Does he have a good sense of humor? Does it keep him out of trouble when he forgets to bring his science report to school? What does he want? What does he need? His personality, his approach to tackling a problem will decide how the mystery is going to be solved. Quite often, in working out the idea for a mystery, my thoughts begin with a situation, a setting, or an unusual idea, and I have to develop my main character to fit this plan.

As the main character takes shape in my mind, other characters come crowding in, pieces of dialogue suddenly pop into my head, scenes of action start describing themselves, and I know it's time to get ready to chart my novel.

Planning and research

There is really no one correct way to plan a book. Writers have their individual systems, with which they work comfortably. Some writers are very tidy, keeping notes that are properly filed, while others would find that system so tedious it would keep them from ever attempting to write. I'll describe what I do, showing what works best for me. It might be a system that will work for other writers, too.

I mentioned that the idea for *The Mystery of the Secret Stowaway* grew from a setting—a luxury liner at sea. Before the story could begin to take shape, I had to do some research. With some of my books, the research has included the study of peoples and customs, of occupations and of places; but with *Secret Stowaway,* the beginning research was concerned only with the setting itself: the deck plan of the liner. I visited a travel agency and looked through their brochures until I found exactly what I wanted—a brochure with the complete deck plan laid out in detail.

This deck plan served two purposes: It gave me the information I needed about the plan of the ship, and it provided me with a map on which I could later place my characters, by assigning them staterooms. The map is a memory prod. Although I had been on similar ships, I knew my memory would be faulty when it came to details such as whether the boat deck is higher than the promenade deck, where the laundry room is, or even the office of the ship's doctor. I fastened this deck plan to the wall next to my typewriter, where I could easily refer to it.

I began to develop my characters. My main character I already had in mind: a boy of about eleven, a freckle-faced, red-haired boy. I named him Joe Riley. I didn't want him to set a bad example to readers by stowing away on purpose, so I had to come up with an idea that would keep him on board, but not by choice. Perhaps he could think he overhears a murder being planned and is afraid to come out of his hiding place, not knowing what might happen to him if the plotters discover his presence. Would it be a real murder being planned? A misunderstanding? I'd have to work this point out.

But first—here was a nice, normal eleven-year-old boy who had never been on a luxury liner before and was obviously there without his parents. How would this come about?

It's difficult to explain how certain ideas take form. Occasionally they burst into full bloom, and sometimes they are agonizingly labored over. In this case, the story idea worked out fairly easily. Joe would be on the liner out of curiosity. How would he get aboard? Suppose there was a large family of red-haired, freckle-faced children traveling with their parents, and Joe just joined the pushing, pulling, chattering swarm and came on board unnoticed. How could this happen? I decided that the father of the family planned to give the mother a well-earned rest and had hired a teenage babysitter to keep an eye on the children. The babysitter has just recently met the family, isn't familiar with the children, and fails to notice that an extra child has joined the group.

The "why" came up next. Why was Joe able to be down at the docks without parental supervision? Where were his own parents? I placed Joe with a Mrs. Crumbacher and her annoying daughter, Cissy. He is staying with them while his father, who works as a technician with a movie company, is away on location in Mexico. Joe's mother died a few years ago, and he still misses her. He is a lonely boy, for the moment with no parents. Unable to tolerate Cissy's teasing much longer, he unconsciously gets himself into trouble with Mrs. Crumbacher.

Now to develop the mystery itself, and decide who is going to be the villain in the story. What kind of mystery could develop on board a ship? A plot could go in any one of several directions, all equally mysterious. How about one that is the reverse of Joe Riley's situation? He is on a ship, where he should not be, trying to keep from being discovered. Imagine, on the other hand, that someone was supposed to be on board and wasn't, but had disappeared sometime after the ship had left the dock?

From this idea grew Mr. Riggle, a businessman who makes a fuss when boarding, because his secretary's name has not been checked off the passenger list as already aboard. Yet, he insists, he had waved to her as she stood on an upper deck, just a few moments before, as he came up the gangplank. Does the secretary disappear? No, she shows up later, austere and unfriendly. But Mr. Riggle himself fails to appear for breakfast the first day out at sea, and there is no sign of how or why he disappeared—only a hysterical secretary, demanding that Mr. Riggle be found.

The personal problem would enter the story before the mystery: Joe's loneliness, missing his father; his inability to stay out of trouble with Mrs. Crumbacher no matter how hard he tries—Joe's personal problem would develop immediately, whereas the mystery couldn't begin to take place until Joe was on board the ship.

It was time to put some of these ideas into writing. At the top of the first page of a large, lined legal-sized notepad, I wrote a tentative title. The actual title of the book would come later.

How long should it be? Books for the eight-to-twelve age group vary in length, but the usual length is 26,000 to 30,000 words. A typewritten first draft, with about 300 words per page, would make the manuscript about 100 pages long. The mystery novel would be divided into chapters—usually ten to fifteen work out well for a book of this length.

With *The Mystery of the Secret Stowaway* I began to list my characters on the first page of the notepad. My main character I knew well by this time, but I needed to visualize and jot down quick descriptions of others who cropped up. When a minor character comes into a book in chapter three and is not seen again until chapter seven, it's often difficult for the author to remember if that character is tall and bald, or short and fat with fuzzy blond hair. This is where the list comes in. It may never be necessary to state in the book that the ship's captain has green eyes, but it's nice to have this fact jotted down just in case you need to use it.

The red-haired family was named Handy. I knew they would play an important part in the story, since obviously Joe would need to eat and have a place to stay on the ship while the mystery was being solved. One particular family member came into being. She was a girl near Joe's age—a bossy girl, used to bullying her younger brothers and sisters. She could be a help to Joe, and also a hindrance, and she could provide some of the humorous elements in the story. I called her Harriet.

Here is an example of how I listed a few of my characters:

> *Harriet Handy*—near Joe's age, 10½. Plump with fuzzy red hair and freckles. Drives her twin brother crazy, and is leader in her family, whether the other children like it or not. Has an active imagination.
>
> *Dodi*—movie starlet, blonde, big blue eyes, beautiful. Not too bright, but very kind. Doesn't like the blue poodle she is always photographed with, but is trying to play a part to suit her agent. Is amiable to a point, enjoys relaxing when the agent isn't around. Entertains as singer on ship. Wants to be an actress, but is terrible. Sings well, however.
>
> *Jerry*—agent, nervous, easily excitable, plump, short man. Gray appearance, in clothes, hair, face (a little baggy with dark smudges under eyes). Trying to push Dodi into being an actress.

On the second page, at the top, I put the words: CHAPTER ONE. Although the chapters in books for the eight-to-twelve age group are usually given titles, I work these out after the book is written. Often a good chapter title will come from a line in that chapter, but it's important not to have the title give away the secret of that chapter.

Linked units

What exactly is a chapter? What will it need to include? A chapter is one of the several sections of the book which carry the story to its climax and solution. Each chapter contains an episode of the story's action, ties in with the chapter preceding it, and leads into the chapter following it. Each chapter brings the reader closer and closer to the climax. Something must happen to the main character of the story in each chapter—something that will change his situation in some way. It can involve a change in attitude, or in his relationship with other characters. It can mean he is closer to danger or more involved in the mystery, whatever the author chooses; by the time the chapter ends, the character will find himself in slightly or radically different circumstances. And, of course, since this is a mystery novel, it is important to have a "cliff hanger" ending for each chapter: an unsolved question that will demand that the reader begin reading the next chapter to find the answer.

In my large notepad, under CHAPTER ONE, I jotted down ideas I felt should be in the beginning of the story. These ideas were not necessarily written in an orderly fashion. Some of the sentences were not even complete. But I established my main character and launched him into the action.

In the margin, I wrote the day that particular action was taking place—Tuesday, for example—so I could use this as a reference point and not forget the day of the week on which the action was taking place. In some chapters, I often put the time of day, too, especially if the action in three or four chapters occurs on the same day.

My notes began with the words: "Joe is in trouble with Mrs. Crumbacher and her daughter, Cissy." Then, ideas about how Joe, feeling lonely, rides around Los Angeles on a bus, ending up at the downtown terminal where he catches a bus for Wilmington. He walks from the end of the line to the docks to see the ship. He gets on board, as planned, by joining the large, noisy Handy family, so that he is unnoticed by the ship's officer who stands at the top of the gangplank. In my notes, Joe begins to explore the ship, overhears what he thinks is the murder, ending with these words: "Whistle sounds, sounds again. Joe finally realizes the ship is moving. He's a stowaway!"

When it came to writing, I realized I had too much material for one chapter, so I broke it in two. That sentence beginning, "Joe is in trouble with Mrs. Crumbacher . . ." became a chapter all to itself, showing just how Joe got into trouble, establishing his character, the setting and problem, and throwing him into immediate action.

Each page thereafter was given a chapter number as heading. Whenever I chart a juvenile mystery novel, I work out the ending soon after I have decided on the beginning, often skipping to this last chapter to outline what I want in it. Then I begin to fill in the other chapters, going back to Chapter Two and moving the story toward the climax and ending.

The climax of the story is the highest point in the action—a moment when the main character has his back to the wall; everything depends on his solution of the mystery and exposure of the villain, and how well he can carry it off.

In *Secret Stowaway*, Joe literally has his back to the wall after being cornered in the kennels by the irate secretary, Miss Stanhope, who is aware that Joe knows too much to let him go. Fortunately, Joe has asked the young man operating the kennels to call the captain. So the captain arrives, and Joe hears Miss Stanhope order the captain to "lock up this stowaway!" It's now or never, and Joe, with the help of the poodle, Feef, unmasks Miss Stanhope as the real Mr. Riggle in disguise—a man who has embezzled bonds from his bank and is trying to get away with the crime by staging his own disappearance at sea.

The ending, Chapter Twelve, consisted of just a few pages, solving Joe's personal problem, reuniting Joe with his father, and tying up the loose ends. Joe has solved the mystery itself at the climax in the last pages of Chapter Eleven.

I keep the plan of my story loose, so that I can make changes in subplots and even in the major story line, because sometimes as I write I think of a better direction to take. Usually, however, in writing the mystery story, it's best to stay fairly close to my basic plot, because all the clues, plants, action, and interaction that form the solution to the mystery are closely interwoven. If the plot is changed too much, then all these factors must change, too, and that can get complicated for the writer.

Subplots begin to take shape as the book is being charted. Dodi, the night club singer, began to emerge as more than just a minor character in the story. Joe needed another friend besides Harriet—an adult friend—and I began to see that Dodi needed a friend, too—someone who would be as completely honest with her as an eleven-year-old boy could be. Dodi was already established as a terrific singer, but a mediocre actress. However, she tried to please Jerry, her agent, by heading her career in what was the wrong direction for her talent. Joe was able to help Dodi understand, through the progress of the story, that she should make the most of her singing talent and enjoy being a singer, instead of trying so hard and so unhappily to be an actress— something she can't do well. Through Joe, Dodi gained the self-confidence to express her own wishes to Jerry.

Here is exactly what I included on the page under the heading, CHAPTER THREE, on my chart, with "Tuesday" again written in the margin:

Joe takes Fifi for walk. (Calls her "Feef") Comes around corner and nearly runs into Riggle again. Riggle nervous and angry and kicks at Feef, causing dog to cry out in pain. (Note: This is a plant that is important later in the solution of the mystery.) Makes Joe angry. He takes Feef to get her dinner and get settled in kennel.

Joe begins to wonder about his own dinner. Finds out that he has to have assigned seat in dining room. Begins to wonder if he can get along on nothing but candy bars.

Noisy Handy family comes along with teen-age babysitter going crazy. Hears her tell woman that she took the job to have a sea cruise, then found out they had eight children. One boy— ten years old—is seasick and won't be down to dinner. Joe takes youngest girl's hand again and follows right along into dining room. Children don't give him away . . . . work out reason why.

Ten-year-old girl, Harriet, sits next to him and wants to know who he is and what he's doing there. Won't believe any of the stories he tells her. Finally makes up a story of her own about his being a spy and tells her younger brothers and sisters not to give it away. Teen-age babysitter is too exhausted and busy to notice he doesn't belong with them, and parents are at another table so that mother can get a rest.

In writing this chapter, I established the reason the little children accepted Joe's presence (thinking Harriet is playing a trick on the babysitter), and changed the fact that Harriet thought Joe was a spy to her thinking he's a runaway being followed by the police, with Joe encouraging her to believe this for his own purposes.

New twists and turns

While you're charting a book is the time to discover if the story line is thin. If you are not able to develop a good piece of action in each chapter, then you're missing something. The answer is not in "padding" the book with extra dialogue or description, or sidetracked action that doesn't move the story along, because the use of these would lead to a dull story. The answer often comes from thinking up a new twist for the plot or a new development concerning an additional character brought into the action—something that will enhance the story line and make the central plot stronger.

When writing a juvenile mystery novel, read the plan or chart of the book carefully, making sure that all the loose ends are taken care of and that all the plants and clues are in their proper places. Then begin the first draft.

I like to work on one chapter at a time, to go through it full of enthusiasm, not worrying about spelling or a particular word or looking up a reference I may not be sure of. I simply put a red pencil check at any point I want to question later, and keep going. When I've finished the chapter, I read it aloud to myself, and that's where I catch many errors. The eye alone might not notice that the same word is used four times in one paragraph, but the ear may pick it up right away. I rewrite, polish, and try to get that chapter into the best shape I can before moving on to the next one.

When I've written all my chapters, I go over the whole manuscript at one, uninterrupted time, making further changes and polishing it till I'm happy with my efforts and ready to type it and send it to a publisher. This rewriting and polishing, over and over again, is one of the most important aspects of writing a book. It's often helpful to use different colored pens when making manuscript changes. I use red, blue, and black—one for immediate changes, one for the overall chapter changes, and one for the last rewrites. This helps me evaluate the progression of rewriting in the manuscript.

The time between writing chapters, when my mind must be occupied with other things, occasionally takes me out of the mood of the book. I've found that what is most helpful is utilizing my subconscious. I read over what I have already written—at least the last chapter—and go over the plan of the next chapter before I go to sleep at night. In the morning, I am usually full of enthusiasm and eager to get back to work on the book.

3

Plotting

ONE OF the most difficult tasks in learning to write fiction is learning how to plot. Many beginning writers get manuscripts back with notations on the rejection slips stating, "Story is too slight," and they groan, "But what does the editor mean by 'too slight'?"

What the editor usually means is that the story doesn't have enough plot. And plot means that a character must have a problem and solve it. But often incident is confused with plot. For example:

Suppose someone wants to write a story about a boy— Jack—whose parents have just been transferred to a city where they have never lived before. The personal problem is that Jack has no friends and wants to make some. The mystery angle involves the stealing of some checks from the apartment house mailboxes. Suppose Jack meets another boy in the lobby of the apartment house and finds out that some mail has been stolen the previous day. Jack then remembers seeing a man at the mailboxes and describes him; the man he describes is known in the neighborhood. The boys inform the police, the mystery is solved, and the boys become friends.

What makes this only an incident? The character does almost nothing to solve the problem himself. What he has done is accidental. He merely lets things happen to him, and there is no reason for the reader to cheer him on, to worry along with him, to feel any suspense about what might happen to him or to take pleasure in the solution. There is no real question regarding the mystery and how it will be solved.

On the other hand, suppose Jack does or says just the wrong thing when he meets the other boy—something that would turn his would-be friend against him? Maybe in his desperation to make a friend he brags or shows off. Now he has a real problem, and it looks as though he'll have great difficulty solving it. He can become more involved in the mystery if something in the stolen mail is of tremendous value or importance to his parents. He has no idea who has rifled the mailboxes, but he wants to find out, to prove himself—especially to the boy in the building who feels animosity toward him instead of friendship. Perhaps the boy could actually get in Jack's way, hindering his efforts, or even suspect Jack of being the thief. The plot of the story will be concerned with Jack's efforts to solve the mystery, his failures, and his eventual success in solving both the mystery and his personal problem.

Important goals

Sometimes "too slight" may mean that the goal the character sets is too trivial. When the goal is unimportant, the author may have touched only on the beginning of the story possibilities and not gone on to develop them fully. Only if the goal is important to the main character will it be important to the reader as well.

Aside from the obvious goal of simply solving the mystery, what types of goals have authors used effectively? In one recent juvenile mystery novel, a young girl has struggled to save a friend from being sent to a home for the insane; in another, a boy has tried everything—including a desperate appeal to someone who can help with black magic—to keep his sister from being lured into the sea by the Great Selkie. In still another novel, a girl has worked to prevent her grandfather from being dispossessed from the home he loves.

Having the main character himself (or herself) solve the problem in the juvenile mystery novel should be accomplished with a great deal of action throughout the plot. Characters must be in motion. The author should change the locale from scene to scene, so the characters are not confined to one place as they solve the mystery, and each scene should contain a sense of movement and physical action.

Even in *The Mystery of the Secret Stowaway,* in which Joe Riley is confined to one location through most of the book—the ship on which he has stowed away—there is a great deal of action and shifts of scene. The characters move about the ship, and a chase scene that takes up most of one chapter leads to the climax and involves not only the villain, but two other characters, who are after Joe Riley. There are scenes in which Joe is trying to dodge Harriet, and scenes in which Harriet and Joe are spying on Miss Stanhope. Characters in a mystery don't just sit and chat. They are on their feet and moving!

Successful authors consistently give this advice: *Show* the story happening; don't *tell* about it. The story is made up of scenes with transitions linking them together, and it is in these scenes that the story is shown taking place.

Scenes as plot units

A scene is a unit of plot carrying the high points in the action of the story, and any short story or novel consists of a series of scenes leading to a climax. They vary in length, depending on what the author wants to show in each. Too many short scenes can make a story seem choppy and confusing; on the other hand, except for a short-short story perhaps, it would be quite difficult to develop a mystery fully in only one scene.

When writers plan their scenes—and they should think their stories through in scenes before and while they are doing the actual writing—they must think of the conflict involved, because every scene should have some conflict, physical or mental. This conflict should move the story along toward its climax.

Conflict is essential to plot. It intensifies the main problem, adds new complications to the central problem, and helps to develop that character by the way he, or she, handles the conflicts that arise. For example, conflict was used in this scene from *The Mystery of the Secret Stowaway* to add suspense and danger, and to plant a needed clue:

> It was fun to go around the promenade. Feef was really perking along, and I was walking faster and faster. I guess we went around a corner too quickly, because Feef and I ran right into that guy with the beard—Mr. Riggle.
>
> He glared at me, and before I knew what he was up to, he hauled off and kicked Feef out of the way. She yipped and whimpered and ran behind me to hide.
>
> "Hey!" I yelled. "You kicked my dog!"
>
> "I did not," he said. "I merely moved it out of the way."
>
> "But you hurt her!"
>
> He didn't even answer. He just nudged past me, pushing me against the wall. I picked up Feef, and we watched Mr. Riggle charging down the promenade. He was about the meanest man I'd ever run into. I had the creepy feeling that I was going to meet up with him again and that the next time there was going to be real trouble.

No scenes should end completely resolved. They should create new problems or possible hope for solutions that seem impossible; and they should lead the reader toward the next scene so that interest isn't lost.

A scene should involve an emotion in the character's situation. The location doesn't matter; it can change a number of times during one scene, for the emotional conflict the character is going through is what determines the scene. A scene in a story or novel differs in this respect from a scene in a play, which is limited as to what can be shown in one setting before the curtain falls.

For example, one scene of *The Mystery of the Secret Stowaway* takes place in a corridor of a ship, in a stateroom, and then back through the corridor and up the stairs—all with action and dialogue going on throughout.

Visualizing actions and emotions

Scenes should be intensely visual. The reader must be able to see what is happening and feel the same emotions the characters are feeling. Authors are in control of their readers' emotions from the beginning to the end of the mystery novel, and they exercise that control by expressing the emotions of their main characters so vividly and visually that their readers identify completely and share the story with the main character.

Each scene will be different in structure, depending upon its purpose in the novel. Some scenes will show the development of the main character or his reaction to his surroundings. Some scenes will be fast-paced, filled with physical action. As the plot builds toward its climax, the pace will be accelerated, the problem will be intensified, and the main character will be increasingly concerned about the barriers he must overcome to achieve his goal.

To accelerate the pace, use more strong action verbs and shorter sentences, increase the action, and keep readers aware of the intensified emotional state of the main characters.

In setting up the scenes that go together to produce a

chapter, it's necessary for me to go through the notes I've made under a chapter heading to try to visualize which pieces of action will make strong scenes, and which can be minimized and used simply as transitions.

For example, in Chapter Six of *The Mystery of the Secret Stowaway,* I wanted to begin with Joe's reactions after he had seen Mr. Riggle throw a package overboard at the end of Chapter Five. Since Joe was alone, and his reaction consisted merely of wondering what Mr. Riggle was doing, I made it a short scene of two paragraphs, adding a transition which took him off the upper deck and into the corridor outside the Handys' staterooms.

Now a longer scene was needed to accomplish a number of things, as Joe goes to the Handy boys' stateroom to spend the night: showing more of Joe's strength of character as he proves he isn't afraid of Harriet and doesn't intend to follow her orders; giving the reader information about the Handy boys and their big sister's bullying; adding a moment of quick suspense, as Joe knocks on the wrong door and nearly blows the whole thing; providing conflict between Joe and Betty Francis, the babysitter; and, of course, moving the plot of the story along.

I went directly into a scene that took place the next morning, after a short transition. In this scene, the conflict switches to Joe versus Harriet, as she tries to tell him what to do, and even threatens to get her own way. Joe stands his ground, wins an encounter, and shows sympathy for Frank, Harriet's seasick twin. It's a short scene, and leads into one in the public men's room, where Joe goes to comb his hair.

This fourth scene is just two paragraphs long, describing how Joe combs sand out of his hair onto a ledge under the mirror. He's not surprised the sand is there, since he apparently hasn't thoroughly combed his hair since the day before, when he and some friends "got to wrassling around in

the sand box at school." Just for fun, Joe pushes the sand
into the shape of a small arrow and then goes to join the
others for breakfast. That arrow provided a false clue for
the captain and the people on the ship who will soon be
searching for the missing Mr. Riggle, and also adds a complication for Joe, who is in enough trouble already.

In the next scene, in the ship's dining room, Joe is an
observer, as a nervous Miss Stanhope informs a waiter that
Mr. Riggle has failed to meet her for breakfast, yet he
wasn't in his stateroom. Joe has an argument with Harriet,
as he scolds her for saying unkind things about Miss Stanhope's ugliness and thick ankles—a plant that will tie into
Joe's eventual realization that Miss Stanhope is really Mr.
Riggle in disguise.

A transition takes Joe and Harriet out of the dining room
and down a corridor, where they overhear information
about Mr. Riggle's disappearance from the ship—the first
they have known about it. In this short scene they question
the women, who gladly tell them everything they have
heard. In this way the information can be given through
dialogue, which brings the reader right into the action instead of telling about it.

In the seventh scene, Joe takes Harriet to a quiet place on
the ship, where they won't be interrupted, and tells her
about seeing Mr. Riggle and the package. They try to decide
what happened. Harriet thinks Mr. Riggle was murdered and
thrown overboard; Joe thinks that's a wild idea, but can't
come up with another explanation. They decide not to tell
anyone yet about what Joe saw, because of his dangerous
position as stowaway. They plan to keep watching people to
see if they notice something else that might be suspicious.
This scene is needed to give information and set up the
beginning of Joe's detecting. An element of worry is introduced, and Joe's illegal status on the ship causes a real
complication.

In the transition that follows this scene, Joe and Harriet part. In the next scene, Joe brings Feef up to the deck for a walk and has a slight run-in with the attendant bringing the cart with the mid-morning rolls and soup to the passengers. This short passage in the scene provides not only conflict but humor in the exchange of dialogue. Miss Stanhope comes bursting from the corridor, some ships' officers with her. She is in a frantic state, and the officers try to calm her down. Feef reacts by hiding under the deck chair and growling. Joe picks her up and says, "What's got into you, Feef? You have better manners than that." Here is another clue—Feef has recognized the man who kicked her, even though he is now disguised as Miss Stanhope.

Joe continues his walk with Feef in a one-paragraph transition of description, and as he gets into the elevator with her, another scene begins. It's a very short scene in which Joe overhears other passengers discussing the missing Mr. Riggle, and the "clue" in the form of the arrow made of sand. This scene ends the chapter by providing information through dialogue and making Joe realize he is in more trouble as he thinks: "One more complication. This guy Riggle—wherever he was, or wasn't—had started to haunt me!"

This was a fairly long chapter in the book, consisting of nine scenes, a total of about 3000 words. In contrast, Chapter Eight has only three scenes, shown in about 1800 words.

Complications and unsolved questions

Suspense must be sustained throughout the plot of the juvenile mystery if the reader is to be kept interested. Suspense means keeping readers guessing, keeping them curious. If readers know how a book will end, they aren't likely to finish it; so writers must use their ingenuity to create complications in the plot for their main characters, to make their efforts to solve the mystery temporarily fail or back-fire or take a sudden, unexpected turn for the worse. These complications, which develop the plot of the story, are the key to maintaining suspense.

In the juvenile mystery these complications usually have to do with possible danger, threats, occult happenings, or characters who try to prevent the main character from solving the mystery.

One technique that helps maintain suspense in the mystery is to end each chapter with an unsolved question. It can be something puzzling or downright frightening, and is designed to pull the reader into the next chapter. This type of ending, as I mentioned earlier, is called a "cliff hanger." This example is from a chapter in *The Mysterious Red Tape Gang:*

> Linda Jean grabbed my arm and squeezed so tightly that the pressure of her fingers was painful. "Mike!" she whispered, "those men might hurt my father!"
>
> The same thought had occurred to me. I wanted to answer her, but my mouth was dry, and I tried to swallow.
>
> Mr. Hartwell's face looked awful. He was like a trapped animal.
>
> "Mike!" Linda Jean whispered. "You've got to do something!"

Suspense can be achieved in a number of other ways. In *The Mystery of Hurricane Castle,* the frightening old stone house, complete with a ghost that might appear at any moment, created the suspense. In *Death at Their Heels,* by Margaret Goff Clark, the suspense centered on the unseen persons who are trying to find Denny's older brother, Rick, who knows only that these men want to take his life and he must escape.

The time element is often used as an effective device in maintaining suspense throughout a plot. In *A Stranger Came*

Ashore, by Mollie Hunter, Robbie is working against time—a definite date—in trying to save his sister from the Great Selkie. In *The Frightened Forest,* by Ann Turnbull, a strange, occult mood surrounds the whole novel, as a witch-like power captures the countryside. This eerie atmosphere creates much of the suspense.

The writer should not try to sustain tension throughout the book, no matter how adventure-filled the story may be. Periods of excitement should be balanced with quieter scenes to give readers a chance to catch their breath. For example, a little light humor can successfully break up the more frightening, intense moments in the juvenile mystery. However, even these less tense scenes should move the story along and not allow it to slow in interest.

Chapter Eight in *The Mystery of the Secret Stowaway* is concerned with Joe's suspicions of Miss Stanhope and his decision to try to discover more about her. Between the times when he and Harriet spy on Miss Stanhope and their fear that she has overheard them and knows what they are doing, I wanted something light to break the serious mood:

> I was passing a deck chair, when a voice said, "Psst, Joe. Sit down here—next to me."
>
> There was Harriet lying in a deck chair with a newspaper over her face, looking like someone who had gone to sleep in the sun. Only she had made two little holes in the paper to look through. At a distance it was all right, but if you looked closely it was creepy, because one hole was poked right into the face of a horse, and here was this blue eye going around and around.
>
> "That's a crazy trick," I told her, sitting down.
>
> "Talk out of the corner of your mouth," she said, "so no one will know you're talking to me."
>
> "I will not," I said. "I'm not going to talk at all. I'm going to eat. I'm hungry."
>
> "Then I'll talk to you," she said. And wouldn't you know it, the first thing she said was a question, so I had to answer.
>
> "Are you sure you weren't telling a big, big fib about Mr.

Riggle throwing something overboard?"

I was so surprised I stopped eating. "Why do you ask a dumb question like that? I was telling the truth."

The newspaper nodded up and down. "All right then," she said. "That just makes everything more suspicious."

"Why?"

"Because," she said, "I overheard Miss Stanhope telling one of the ship's officers that not a thing of Mr. Riggle's was missing, except the clothes he was wearing."

"That's strange," I said.

"You don't suppose he could have been . . . well, standing at the rail with nothing on, throwing his clothes overboard?"

"Harriet!" I said. "Don't you think that's something I would have noticed?"

"It was just a wild guess."

Subplots and plants

In any mystery novel the mystery is introduced near the beginning and runs throughout the book, remaining unsolved until the end, as does the main character's personal problem. But there will be other problems that crop up in the story, minor problems which add to the overall suspense and which are often solved within a few chapters, a few pages, or even a few paragraphs. These are the subplots, and they must always be in some way related to the main character, even though they may involve minor characters. Some subplots will tie in so closely with the central plot that they cannot be solved until the central problem is solved.

Sometimes a minor character will not enter the story until later in the book, but if he or she is important to the plot and can't be introduced immediately, it's often a good idea to hint at his or her existence in the opening paragraphs of the story. If a character is crucial to the solution of the mystery, he shouldn't be brought in at the last moment, because this is confusing to the reader. Even if there is no need for him or her in the first part of the mystery story, the existence of such a person should be planted early. A good example of this is found in Richard Peck's *The Ghost Belonged to Me.* In the second paragraph of the novel, in a discussion about ghosts, Alexander refers to his great-uncle, Miles Armsworth, though Uncle Miles doesn't appear until the fourth chapter. But he is an essential character in the story, and by the time he enters it, the reader is expecting him.

A juvenile mystery writer must plant other items of information as well. If the main character is going to discover that the secret to the mystery lies in a priceless antique teapot, then it's essential to plant that teapot near the beginning of the story and even refer to it elsewhere in some way that won't make readers suspicious.

The planting doesn't have to tie in with the final solution of the mystery. It can be used in connection with events that appear in other parts of the story. For example, in Chapter Two of *The Mysterious Red Tape Gang,* the boys are secretly preparing to move Mr. Hartwell's hibiscus bush, and a plant is needed:

> I had put the pruning shears in the clubhouse, and I felt around in the dark until I found them. "I've got the pruning shears right here."
>
> Tommy felt them. "Are those ours? My dad's been griping at me, 'cause he can't find ours, and he thinks I had something to do with their being missing."
>
> "No," I said. "They're ours. My dad puts his name on everything he owns."
>
> "I know why too," Leroy said. "Because when you left his hoe and rake over in the parkway and . . ."

Two things were set up in this plant: the shears had Mike's father's name on them; and Mike had previously been careless of things belonging to his father. When, in the confusion of hurrying from the Hartwell home in the middle of the night, the shears get left behind, the reader can accept it. And when, in the next chapter, Linda Jean Hartwell blackmails herself into the boys' club with the incriminating pruning shears she found and kept secretly, again it makes sense to the reader. I needed Linda Jean in the club, and this was what I came up with to help her become accepted as a member. If the boys had merely thought it over, had a change of heart, and invited her to join without a threat hanging over their heads, few, if any, young readers would have believed it.

Sub-mysteries are used to aid suspense in the juvenile mystery novel. A sudden glimpse of what might be a ghost, but is logically accounted for a few pages later; a mysterious shadow that appears and reappears but is explained before the end of the main mystery—such sub-mysteries add much to the suspense of the juvenile mystery and are necessary to round out the plot. Real clues, false clues (or red herrings), and hidden clues should be planted throughout the story, not only to create suspense, but to make the ending fit into place neatly. Red herrings, by the way, are fun for the author to sneak into the story line; and young readers expect them, ready to try to decide if they are real clues or not. Each false clue must have a logical explanation, however, and not be left dangling.

It is never fair for the author to withhold clues from the reader in order to make the ending a complete surprise. Mystery fans like to see if they can solve the mystery along with the main character or protagonist—better yet, even before. And they love clues that they see immediately, but the main character misses. The clues should be difficult, so that the readers may not catch them in a quick reading, but they should still be in plain sight.

Guidelines for plotting

The following questions, along with my "answers" for *The Mystery of the Secret Stowaway*, will give you a guideline to follow in plotting your mystery.

1. *What will the central mystery in the novel be? Is it a strong mystery, believable, and something a young person could understand and take interest in?*

The central mystery in *The Mystery of the Secret Stowaway* is the disappearance of Mr. Riggle from a ship at sea.

2. *Does the mystery contain the essential elements of fear and possible danger?*

These elements evolve from the question of where Mr. Riggle could be, if he is still somewhere on the ship; and from the danger Joe feels as he begins to uncover the clues and come closer to the solution of the mystery.

3. *What main character can handle the solution of this mystery? Can he take care of it by himself? Will he need help from friends his age or from adults? Will readers relate to this main character?*

Joe Riley is the main character who will solve the mystery. Although his decisions and actions shape the solution of the mystery, he can't solve it entirely by himself, but will need help from adults. The story will become more interesting if he gets "help"—sometimes unwanted—from a character his own age—Harriet.

4. *Who is the antagonist in the story? Is there more than one? Is there a character acting against the main character, and is the main character also facing opposition from himself through his own fear or shyness?*

The antagonist in the story is Mr. Riggle. However, there is more than one physical antagonist. Jerry, the agent, dislikes Joe; and Frank, Harriet's seasick brother, is another "enemy" who resents Joe's taking his place in the dining room. Joe is up to facing each situation that arises and is not acting against himself.

5. *What is the main character's personal problem that must run through the story—one that he will solve close to*

*the climax of the book? Is it a strong, believable one that
will hold the readers' interest?*

Joe's personal problem is his loneliness for his parents,
and this leads to his tendency to get himself into trouble. A
child missing his parents and being blamed for things he
doesn't do on purpose are problems to which young readers
can relate.

6. *Does the main character consistently work toward the
climax, meeting obstacles along the way that make it seem
harder—or even impossible—to reach the goal, or solution of
the mystery?*

The climax of this story occurs when the antagonist is
unmasked, endangering Joe. The situations that arise in
which he can't find the proof he needs, or is threatened, or
is about to be exposed as a stowaway—these and others
interfere with his reaching the goal of solving the mystery.

7. *Is there plenty of conflict throughout the book which
involves the main character with the antagonist and with
other characters?*

The conflict involves Joe versus Mrs. Crumbacher and
Cissy, Joe versus Harriet, Joe versus Jerry, Joe versus the
babysitter, Joe versus Frank, and Joe versus Miss Stan-
hope/Mr. Riggle.

8. *Is there plenty of action, so that the characters are
moving as they are talking, or are involved in some physical
activity?*

There is action all over the ship, with Joe in various
places and situations that call for physical movement.

9. *Is suspense utilized in every way possible to create
scenes that make readers hold their breath, fearful of the
outcome?*

There are scenes in which a time element creates suspense; scenes in which the reader fears that Joe will not be
allowed to explain and the villain will get away with his
plan; scenes in which Joe is almost discovered as a stow-

away; and scenes in which Joe is in physical danger.

10. *Are there sub-mysteries that lead readers into frightening situations, but are solved before the climax is reached?*

A number of short sub-mysteries are used, and a longer one involves Dodi as a victim of burglary.

11. *Are subplots developed through some of the minor characters? Does their effect on the main character add a third dimension to the characters?*

Two subplots growing through the minor characters are used. Through their relationship with Joe Riley, the Handy children learn they don't have to be intimidated by their big sister, Harriet; and Dodi gets the courage to do what she wants to do most, instead of following Jerry's pattern for her life.

12. *Are there plenty of clues and red herrings to add action and suspense to the plot and lead it toward the climax?*

There are a number of clues, such as Harriet's comment about Miss Stanhope's thick ankles (repeated in a later conversation between Harriet and Dodi); Feef's growling at Miss Stanhope each time she sees her; the package that went overboard; Miss Stanhope's wig; and so forth.

13. *Is the climax one of the most exciting, fast-paced scenes in the book? Is it developed in full, so that readers who have been waiting for this moment can participate in it fully?*

The climax is the biggest scene in *The Mystery of the Secret Stowaway*. Joe is cornered by Miss Stanhope, Jerry and Frank, before he can go to the captain with his suspicions. Even when the captain and Dodi appear, it looks as though Joe won't be able to tell the captain his suspicions about Mr. Riggle, because Frank reveals that Joe is a stowaway. Physical action is used with the dialogue to increase the pace of this scene.

The plot, with all its ingredients—conflict, suspense, action, and a strong problem to be solved by the main character—is of primary importance in the juvenile mystery novel. Juvenile mystery authors may sometimes wish they could dwell more on characterization or descriptions or setting, but their readers demand that they make plotting the focal point of their mystery novels.

4

Characterization

THE MAIN character is one of the most important elements in the mystery story, because the problem of finding the solution to the mystery will be placed firmly into his or her hands. The construction of the plot will depend upon whether the main character is a scatterbrain, a timid soul, or perhaps the kind of person who will recklessly blunder into a situation. He (or she) will solve the mystery in a way that is in keeping with his temperament or personality traits, and it's up to the author to know his character well.

It is also essential for authors to like their main characters, because, if they do not, their feelings will come through as they write about these fictional people, and readers will not like—or be able to relate to—the characters. Children who read mystery novels won't empathize with a cruel main character or one with disagreeable traits. But in the same way, they don't want to identify with a "perfect" character with only good, noble qualities. Young readers want to read about people like themselves: people who get scolded occasionally, because they can't manage to get to school on time or remember to keep their rooms tidy, or who tend to procrastinate or sneak their broccoli to the dog under the table—all minor faults, but they make the characters more human.

Creating "originals"

The main character in a mystery novel must have a distinct personality and must be presented so vividly that readers become interested in him or her at the beginning of the story and want to stick with him until the last word, to make sure that he solves the mystery, as well as his personal problem.

Throughout *The Pencil Families,* by Susan Terris, Emily Mendle pesters her older brother in countless ways, wanting his attention. The things she does to bother him, in her need for love and reassurance from him, take her out of the uninteresting position of little-sister-trying-to-solve-a-mystery, and sharpen the distinctive pictures readers are shown of both Emily and her brother.

Writers should not attempt to reproduce as characters in their books real people they have known in life. They can borrow some of their friends' mannerisms, or ways of speaking, or physical descriptions, or even parts of their names; but the ingredients they use should be mixed with others drawn from their own imaginations, so that the characters they invent are individuals in their own right, not copies of real-life people. Writers then can do with their characters what they wish and not feel constrained to follow a pattern live models have set.

There was a time in which editors preferred stories which featured boys, believing that both boys and girls would read about boys, but only girls would read about girls. Fortunately, these ideas have changed, and girls are just as popular as boys as central characters in the juvenile mystery.

Aside from the main characters in the novel, there is a wide range of people who can be characters in children's mysteries. There are cantankerous old ladies, ex-sailors, spies, spiritualists, musicians, visitors from the past and present—even nobility from various countries—who inhabit some of the current mysteries for young people.

Readers should be able to visualize characters as alive and interesting. One way this can be accomplished is through description. You can give a visual presentation of your characters, always remembering one important fact: Young readers of today are impatient. They want the story to move along at a lively pace. We have long passed the day when authors could devote pages to descriptions of characters with no intervening action. Now, in order to hold our readers' attention, we must interweave description with action, emotion, dialogue, and narrative that will move the story toward the climax.

In *Z for Zachariah,* by Robert C. O'Brien, written in the first person, Ann records the approach of an unknown person into her valley, noting in her journal daily that the smoke from his campfire seems to be coming nearer and nearer. For eighteen pages, the reader is made to wonder who the person or persons might be, until Ann writes the following item (introducing the character through description):

May 24
It is a man, one man alone.
This morning I went as I had planned. I put on my good slacks, took the .22 and hung the binoculars around my neck. I climbed a tree and saw him coming up the road. I could not really see what he looks like, because he is dressed, entirely covered, in a sort of greenish plastic-looking suit. It even covers his head, and there is a glass mask for his eyes—like the wet suits skin divers wear in cold water, only looser and bulkier. Like skin divers, too, he has an air tank on his back. But I could tell it was a man, even though I could not see his face, by his size and the way he moves.
The reason he is coming so slowly is that he is pulling a wagon, a thing about the size of a big trunk mounted on two bicycle wheels. It is covered with the same green plastic as his

suit. It is heavy, and he was having a hard time pulling it up Burden Hill. He stopped to rest every few minutes. He still has about a mile to go to reach the top.

I have to decide what to do.

Descriptions in first or third person

Readers should always be able to visualize the main character. In a story written in third person, the description of the character is usually done in narrative form, such as this opening paragraph from *The Secret of the Elms,* by Daniel P. Mannix:

> The little girl struggled down the steps of the suburban local, dragging her suitcase behind her, and stood looking stolidly around, jostled by the more experienced commuters on their way to the parking lot. She shivered in the chill March wind. Although she was twelve, she was small for her age. She was dressed in a school uniform, consisting of a jumper, blouse and bunchy bloomers, while her pipe-cleaner legs were fitted into skintight black stockings. She wore a maroon school blazer with St. Agatha's embroidered on the vest pocket. She was painfully thin and her skin seemed to be made of wax paper. Her hair was mouse colored and her only striking feature was her eyes: brown and intensely serious. They looked enormous in her pinched, colorless face.

It is more difficult to describe the main character in a story written in first person, because the character is in the position of describing himself or herself. Some techniques have been overdone, such as having the character see herself in a mirror and reporting on what she sees there and how she likes—or doesn't like—her own image. The writer must look for new ways to work in this description, and often it's more effective if woven into the action of the story in short phrases or sentences.

In *The Mystery of the Secret Stowaway,* which is in first person, Joe Riley provides some physical description about himself in this manner:

> We went past the big hospital where I was born, and I had to smile as I remembered how my dad said he'd have known me anywhere, without anybody even telling him which was his baby, because I had red hair and freckles. Mom would giggle and tell him that babies didn't have freckles, but he said they were right underneath, ready to come out, and he could see them even if no one else could.

Characters can also be described to the reader through dialogue. An elderly, well-educated woman will use a different type of speech from that of a gangster; a teen-age girl won't speak like a college president. The dialogue must fit the character, and each character must have his own type of language, mannerisms, expressions, and speech patterns.

Two young characters are involved in this scene from *The Secret of the Disappearing Sultan,* by Margery Warner. One is an American girl, the other a young Arabian sultan near her age. She has discovered him bullying a hotel maid. As they speak to each other, their individual speech patterns are quite distinctive:

> "I don't suppose you speak English," I said, "and I don't think my French is good enough to tell you what I think of you. But," I added grimly, "I am going to try!"
>
> "Let not your tongue cut your throat," said the boy in perfect English. "Instead, I shall tell you what befalls one who enters unbidden into my presence."
>
> "I should approach on my hands and knees, perhaps?"
>
> We glared at each other while he stood at full height.

Readers should know what characters are like through their actions; consistency in action is essential. If the main character in a story is an energetic, athletic girl with a lively curiosity, she'll reveal this personality throughout the book. She'll be vigorous, move rapidly, probably be the leader in a group of other children. Perhaps she'll talk a lot—maybe too much—and be a little too outgoing, so that she stumbles into trouble:

> Patti slammed the screen door behind her, skimmed her books toward the sofa, where they teetered for a moment on the nearest cushion, then plopped to the floor. She shouted, "I'm home! Hey, Mom, I'm home!"
>
> Her mother scurried into the room, making shushing noises. "Your grandpa is here, and he's sleeping," she said.
>
> "Darn! I forgot," Patti said, knowing that even now her voice was too loud. Suddenly she groaned. "Oh, no! I called a meeting of the basketball committee over at our house this afternoon. Everybody will be here!"

With a character depicted this way, a reader wouldn't find it believable if she suddenly became shy, or decided to spend a sunny, Saturday afternoon reading a book. So the character's actions must fit her personality throughout the mystery story.

In *The Case of the Condemned Cat,* by E. W. Hildick, it is established that McGurk is the leader of the detective organization, and Willie is the member who isn't quite as sharp as the others and is more inclined to bungle the job. In this scene near the climax of the story, consistency of character in action creates even more complication in the plot:

> "That cat's far too sweet to be a murderer!" said Wanda quietly.
>
> Her voice broke the spell.
>
> "GRAB HIM!" yelled McGurk.
>
> He made some of us jump.
>
> "That was the idea," he told us afterward. "I could see Mrs. Williams was going to pick Whiskers up. So I yelled like that hoping to scare him off. I didn't really *mean* for anyone to grab him."
>
> Well, it almost worked.
>
> Mrs. Williams was one of those who jumped, and it made her

jerk her arms about just as she was reaching out for the cat.

And Whiskers himself jumped. He stopped rolling on his back, twisted round onto his feet, and looked all set to run away for real.

Then Willie grabbed him. Yes—Willie. Good old Willie.

The Head of the Organization had yelled "Grab him!" and Officer Sandowsky had grabbed.

"If I'd meant it," McGurk complained afterward, "if I'd really wanted that cat caught, if our lives had depended on it—you'd have *missed*!"

Writer empathy

Writers need to use empathy. They must not only know well the characters about whom they are writing, they must be able to place themselves inside these characters' minds— to *become* the characters while the story is going on. They must know how the characters would act in each situation, and why they would behave in that manner—which brings us to motivation.

There must always be a convincing reason for a character's actions. Fictional people should be just as authentic as living people, and when they do something or make a decision or react in a certain way, there should be a reason for it. The author must know these reasons, and the reader deserves to know, too.

There is a double need for sound motivation in the juvenile mystery. The main character's involvement in the mystery must be sufficiently motivated. In the mystery stories for very young children, which have simple plots, the motivation can be nothing stronger than curiosity; but in more involved mysteries for the eight-to-twelve age group and older, there has to be a very good reason why a character would walk into possible trouble or real danger. Authors need to give their characters reasons strong enough and real enough for readers to find them believable.

In *The Wyndcliffe*, by Louise Lawrence, the Hennessy

family moves from London to an ancient house at the edge of the Wyndcliffe. The two teen-age daughters in the family react quite differently. Ruth plunges into the social life of the school and the town, but Anna misses her brother desperately, and she misses her parents who leave for a business trip. She is shy and doesn't get along with Ruth at all. It makes perfect sense that, with her great need for affection, she lets herself fall in love with the handsome young ghost—John Hollis—who inhabits this Wyndcliffe area. Her actions are so well motivated that the reader is actually glad that Anna has found someone who cares about her—ghost or real man.

The Wyndcliffe is also a good example of using contrasts in depicting characters to add conflict to the plot. No two sisters could be less alike—physically or mentally—than Ruth and Anna. When practical Ruth begins to suspect who—or what—Anna is seeing, she reacts by confining Anna to her room and sending for their older brother to help. Ruth means well, but it is painful to Anna to be kept away from John, and the unhappiness it causes leads to a strong climax.

Although writers do not need a formal background in psychology, they should understand some basic rules of human behavior and should be aware of the people they meet and their problems, their actions and reactions, and perhaps come to understand some of the childhood hang-ups that may have shaped their personalities. Studying people you meet every day is one of the best ways to develop the necessary sensitivity and awareness that will help you produce believable characters with sound motivation for their actions.

Series characters

Although many adult mystery novelists have brought

characters to fame through series mysteries, relatively few juvenile mystery writers have done the same. And yet, if you were to ask most adults or children to name a juvenile mystery character, the chances are they would say, "Nancy Drew."

Nancy Drew books are not considered to be top-notch literature by any means, and yet there are countless readers who make it their goal to read every book in the series. Why? Because they relate to Nancy, and they see themselves in her exploits. Nancy has the full attention of her father, a marvelous amount of freedom to do what she wants, an above-average amount of daring and cleverness, and a very satisfying recognition by the local police of her detective talents. The stories fit a format; the solution of the crimes follows a formula; and the plots grow from the main character—what she can do, where she can go, in what situations she can logically be involved.

The problem with series characters in the juvenile field is that they cannot grow or change as the story progresses. Since characters must continue to be the same person at the same age in each of the books in the series, they tend to become stereotyped. There is a handy way to avoid creating a flat, unchanging character of this type, and that is to make the character emotionally involved with a personal problem of his own or that of another character. Another way is to make the main character a little eccentric.

Donald Sobol accomplishes the latter in his *Encyclopedia Brown* stories. Encyclopedia Brown is not like other ten-year-old boys. Although he enjoys the same sports and pastimes they do, he has a fantastic memory for facts and a great sense of deductive reasoning, so that he can solve crimes more easily than even his police chief father. Each book in this series is composed of a number of very short stories—just a few hundred words per story. The reader is invited to try his own skill at deduction, along with Encyclopedia Brown, and the answers to the "puzzle mysteries" are at the back of the book. The stories are a challenge; they are fun to read; and there is no need for the main character to develop or change or show emotional growth as the stories progress. Although the character of Encyclopedia Brown is an interesting one, it is the lure of the mystery, the working out of the clues to find the solution, that is of primary interest to the children who love the Encyclopedia Brown books.

In the true mystery novel, the main character grows or changes in the course of the book. He or she should not be the same at the end of the story as when he first stepped into his adventure. He should have learned something about human nature and at the same time should have solved a problem—his own and possibly that of another person.

Villains

In *The Mysterious Red Tape Gang,* my main character, Michael, and his friends find that the father of Linda Jean, who blackmailed her way into their formerly all-male club, is involved in criminal activities. Even though Mike began the story thinking that Linda Jean was a pain, his loyalties and sympathies are brought into play, and he works to try to help her and her father. As he solves the mystery, his own attitudes change. By the end of the story he has grown emotionally and has become a different person from the uncaring boy he was at the beginning of the story.

How is the villain handled in a mystery novel for this age group? The author must try very hard not to stereotype the antagonist, and sometimes the villain can even be treated with sympathy. There is no reason why the villain should have to be a criminal in the juvenile mystery. Often the villain is a mixed-up contemporary of the main character— perhaps another child in school or in the neighborhood, who is misbehaving and can be straightened out with a little understanding. Sometimes the "villain" can even be such an abstract thing as the main character's own fear of the unknown.

The villain can be depicted in various ways. In *Delbert, the Plainclothes Detective,* I used two villains. One was the man who had robbed Delbert's neighbor and had hoodwinked Delbert. The other was an older boy, Tiger, the bully whom Delbert had suspected of being the criminal. The bully wasn't an intentional villain—at least from his own point of view—and his role as a villain disappeared when Delbert began to understand Tiger's problems:

> Delbert wondered what it would be like to have a mama scared to give you big hugs and tell you that she loved you, and to have a father that yelled at you and yelled at your mama. Delbert began to feel sorry for Tiger . . . Delbert lowered himself to the ground to join Andy. He didn't much like spying on people. He didn't like knowing that Tiger was two people—one the way he had always known him, and one the way he had been at the supper table with his parents.

In other juvenile mysteries, the villain has been a noncorporeal evil, a power no one can actually see, a supernatural force. The villain has been the abstract rules of society; he has been a dangerous criminal, a member of the "syndicate," a witch doctor with a horrible spell, a smuggler.

Adult characters

In nearly every mystery for children, there will be adult characters, and they must be handled carefully. Children read for pleasure, and those readers in the eight-to-twelve age group want to read about other children, not adults who are usually giving them orders or "good advice." Also, the protagonist in the mystery story must solve the problem himself or herself, so authors must keep adults in the background as much as possible—out of the limelight.

Authors have found a variety of ways to make parents leave the scene, such as putting the children in the care of relatives or babysitters who aren't as observant of their behavior (thereby giving the young mystery investigator a chance to operate on his own). Parents can leave town on pleasure trips, take a sick relative to the hospital, or attend an urgent business conference. And children in books can escape the supervision of their parents by visiting relatives in another city, by running away from home, and by accidentally becoming separated from adults during blizzards, hurricanes, or even wars. The new liberated fictional mother can neatly be taken away from the scene of the action, when she goes about her job.

Adult characters in mystery novels for young people should be portrayed as interesting in their own right and should never be made to look ridiculous or foolish in unreal or stereotyped roles. Adults should come into the novel only when their presence is plausible or necessary to the story line or action. At some point near the climax of a mystery novel, the young main character may need to ask his father or mother for help, or even to call the police. Although the story is the young protagonist's, and he should work out the solution to the problem on his own, if it is his decision to seek outside help, then he is still in control of the plot, and the book will retain its believability. Readers will want to step into the shoes of the main character who is going through daring situations calling for bravery, but they have enough sense to recognize that there are times when a twelve-year-old girl can't handle three tough gangsters all by herself, and they are perfectly agreeable to having her call for assistance.

Occasionally, an adult is very important to the story, as in the novel, *The Ghost Belonged to Me,* by Richard Peck, in which the main character's 85-year-old Great-Uncle Miles helps Alexander perform the task the ghost has asked him to do. But even though Uncle Miles takes a strong part in the development of the plot, it is still Alexander who is in control of the story, and his decisions guide it.

Older adults in fiction for children are in a special category, because they have usually lost some of their inhibitions and worries, and don't care a bit if a child eats his lima beans or steps in puddles with his best shoes on. Older people are usually full of good stories, with the time to tell them: children feel a special closeness to them, and they are often highly successful characters in juvenile books. Uncle Miles, for example, has an added advantage as a likable character in that his presence as a carpenter, on a first-name basis with the wealthy families in town, is a great source of discomfort to Alexander's mother, who is a determined social climber for her marriageable daughter's sake. This adds much humor and fun to the story.

When writing for the eight-to-twelve-year-old group, authors usually make their main characters 11, 12, or 13 years old—always near the top of the age group. Children enjoy reading about someone their own age, or a little older than themselves, but they will not relate to a story about a younger child.

Naming your characters

Names should be chosen carefully to "fit" your fictional characters. There are a number of good books of names and their meanings. I often use *What to Name Your Baby*, by Maxwell Nurnberg and Morris Rosenblum. It has a large section of unusual names as well as lists of familiar names for boys and girls. *The New Age Baby Name Book*, by Sue Browder, contains many ethnic names, including American Indian, Swahili, Israeli, Hawaiian, Japanese, and others. It also has a section on how to create a name.

The names selected should not be too difficult to read and pronounce, and they should be dissimilar: never use Jean and Jane or even Richard and Robert in the same book.

A name can perform a secondary duty by describing a character. In Mary Blount Christian's *Goosehill Gang* series, "Tubby" needs no further explanation. And the name for the heroine of *The Frightened Forest,* by Ann Turnbull, Gillian, well suits the mysterious, occult mood of the book; "Debbie" or "Lucy Jane" or "Freckles" wouldn't work at all.

Creating a fully developed main character is one of the most important tasks in writing a publishable juvenile mystery. Readers must become involved in that person's problem and root for his or her success in solving the mystery. Bringing the main character to life, therefore, is one of the author's primary jobs.

5

Dialogue

DIALOGUE in the juvenile mystery has a number of uses aside from aiding in the development of each character. It has the function of helping readers feel they are taking part in the story, too, sharing the drama with the main character.

Without dialogue, the story could only be narrated. With dialogue, the story is *shown taking place;* readers are there on the spot as the story unfolds around them; they *see it* happen. Modern readers enjoy "listening" to the conversation of the characters in a story, and they do not want to get the same information through long paragraphs of description. They want the author to describe the action only when it is necessary, letting the characters' participation in the action be as immediate as possible through dialogue.

Presenting information through dialogue helps readers feel that they are not bystanders but are totally involved in the story. In the following example, dialogue serves a number of purposes:

"I think we should go home!" Sally said. "Mother told us if we were late to dinner again, we'd be in trouble!" [Dialogue gives information reader should know, or hints at a problem that will come up in a later scene.]

"You're just looking for an excuse!" Jack glared at his sister. "You're always getting scared of everything, and you're just too scared to go inside and see why Mr. Allingrod didn't answer the doorbell." [Dialogue gives information about one of the characters—Sally—from Jack's point of view.]

"We've never been inside that creepy old place," Sally said. "The windows are so dirty we can't even see beyond that junk piled on the windowsills." [Dialogue gives information about the setting.]

Jack put a hand on the tarnished doorknob. "I'm going inside. If you don't want to follow me, then don't bother." The doorknob turned easily, and he poked his head into the gloomy room as the door swung open. "Mr. Allingrod!" he called. "Are you all right?" [Dialogue advances the action, moving the plot toward the climax.]

Jack's voice sounded hollow in the empty room. Mr. Allingrod didn't answer.

"You're going to get in trouble," Sally whispered, but she followed Jack closely as he stepped into the room. [Dialogue helps to create suspense.]

"I don't care," Jack said. "Mr. Allingrod?" he called again. [Dialogue tells us something about Jack's character.]

The door suddenly slammed shut behind them!

Conversation with a purpose

Dialogue should be meaningful to the plot in order to move it along effectively. When characters become sidetracked and begin to talk about things not important to the central action and character development, the story comes to a dull standstill.

Suppose Jack hurries to Tom's house after he and Sally find Mr. Allingrod unconscious, and the old man has been taken to the hospital:

"Tom!" Jack pushed past his friend the minute Tom opened the door, and in a rush of words said, "Someone has been in Mr. Allingrod's house! Someone must have been looking for the treasure!"

"You really believe Mr. Allingrod has a 'treasure' hidden in that horrible old place?" Tom asked.

"He said he did."

Tom walked over to the big airchair and dropped into it, sprawling comfortably, with his long legs draped over the side. "I read a book about treasure once," Tom said. "These people went looking for it on one of the little islands in the Caribbean."

"Was it a good book?" Jack asked.

"Pretty good. Want me to tell you what happened in it when these guys ran into some head hunters?"

"I didn't know there were head hunters in the Caribbean," Jack said.

And off on a boring tangent. Suppose, however, that the author uses dialogue to establish Tom as someone who can't keep his mind on anything for long. Then, it could be written like this:

Tom walked over to the big armchair and dropped into it, sprawling comfortably, with his long legs draped over the side. "I read a book about treasure once," Tom said. "These people went looking for it on one of the little islands in the Caribbean and . . ."

"Tom!" Jack interrupted. "There you go again! Can't you pay attention to what I'm saying?"

Tom blinked with surprise. "Pay attention to what?"

"Mr. Allingrod's treasure," Jack said.

"I don't believe in Mr. Allingrod's treasure."

"Well, I do, and I think . . ." Jack looked around quickly and lowered his voice. "I think I know where it is!"

Dialogue should always sound natural—using suitable contractions and broken sentences—coming as close to normal speech patterns as possible. However, writers do have the job of disciplining their characters so that every word they say is useful to the story and interesting to readers.

Of course, occasionally a character might speak in a stilted way. This may be the outstanding characteristic which sets him or her off from the other people in the story. And other characters—to accentuate their individuality—might make a habit of repeating themselves, or speak in monosyllables, or use poor grammar. In any case, the characters' manner of speaking must sound right and natural for them.

In *The Ghost Belonged to Me,* Richard Peck gives each character his own individualized style of speech, and moves the plot along by including in dialogue information that is more interesting there than it would be in narration:

> "Come on in, Uncle Miles, and take a—" Dad caught a glimpse of Mother before he could ask him to sit down. But Gladys slammed through from the kitchen and advanced on him with a beaming face and a cup of coffee.
>
> "Say. Gladys, if I'd a-knowed I'd see you, I'd a-put my teeth in." Uncle Miles fumbled around in his overall pocket and pulled out a full set of false choppers. They grinned out of his fist at Gladys, who whooped a big laugh. Mother shaded her eyes with her hand.
>
> "That will do, Gladys," she moaned.
>
> "Oh, hark at that, Gladys?" said Uncle Miles. "Back to the kitchen while you're still an honest woman. But stay single for me. I'm just a-gettin' into my prime!" Gladys whooped again and vanished.
>
> "Well, Uncle Miles, how you feeling?" Dad said.
>
> "Better'n you look, Joe. You gettin' to look more and more like a pinch-faced banker right along. Settin' at a desk when you'd be better workin' construction in the great out-of-doors. Ain't you laid up enough money yet to suit—"
>
> "Uncle Miles!" Mother said, half out of her chair and her mind. "I want you to remove some of the scrollwork from off the front porch and start thinking about a balustrade for the piazza."
>
> "For the pi—what, Luella?" Uncle Miles turned his spectacles on Mother in surprise.

As the story progresses, it is important that the dialogue seem logical and appropriate to the action and to the character speaking. It must have a point related to the story's development, and readers must be convinced that the characters would say what they do.

In *The Ghost Belonged to Me,* Alexander encounters the young female ghost for the first time, and she warns him that there will be death on the bridge if the "train" is not stopped. Alexander reacts instinctively, realizing that the trolley car from town would pass that way in a few minutes, heading for the trestle over Snake Creek. It must be stopped. The dialogue that takes place after Alexander flags down the trolley shows how each of the characters reacts, in his own, individual, *logical* way:

> "There's trouble on the line," I told him [the conductor], wondering if there was.
> "There'll be trouble for you making mischief!"
> I swung up into the car. He said that as I was entering, I had better have a nickel in my nightshirt. This brought a laugh from the passengers who stared at me a little like I had stared at Inez Dumaine. They all looked to be late workers or people who'd been to a show at the Empress Opera House.
> "That is the Armsworth boy," somebody said, like I was a point of interest they were passing.
> "Off, boy, before I drag you up to your house by the ears," said the motorman, a tough customer with big knuckles.
> I got a good grip on the pole by the coin box. "Listen, there's something wrong on the trestle—over Snake Creek." This brought a few of the passengers to their feet. The motorman pushed his cap back and looked put upon.
> "If this is a prank," he said, "your bottom will burn for it." But the passengers were crowding up front to see if they could read truth in my face.
> One of them said, "Take it easy to the bridge and then have a look."

Dialogue has a visual advantage in that it breaks up a page, making that page look more inviting to young readers. When I was writing *The Mysterious Red Tape Gang,* I could have written a paragraph of narration like this:

> When I finally found the right key to let Leroy out of the locked garage, I almost didn't believe it and nearly lost it again. But I turned the key in the padlock, dropped the keys and the padlock, and jerked the door open. What none of us had thought about was that most businesses are wired with a burglar alarm that has a special door switch, and it went off right in our ears. Leroy came dashing out, and we tried to help Linda Jean find the key ring in the darkness. The police were coming, but I couldn't let Linda Jean go home without those keys. Finally I found them, and we dashed through the loose place in the fence. I could hear the doors of the police car slam, and steps coming closer and closer. If the policeman looked on the other side of the fence, he'd find Linda Jean and me!

However, this is how the action was presented when I wrote the scene, using dialogue to help show the story taking place:

> When I finally found the right key I almost didn't believe it and nearly lost it again.
>
> "Got it," I said. I turned the key in the padlock, dropped the keys and the padlock, and jerked the door open.
>
> What none of us had thought about was that most businesses are wired with a burglar alarm that has a special door switch, and wow, did that thing go off right in our ears!
>
> Leroy came dashing out, yelling, "Run!"
>
> We started off, but Linda Jean grabbed my arm. "Where are the keys?" she screamed.
>
> We all got down on our knees in that alley, trying to find the key ring in the darkness.
>
> Tommy lifted his head. "Oh-oh! Here comes that police car!"
>
> "Make tracks!" Leroy yelled.
>
> "The keys!" I said.
>
> "Forget the keys!" Jimmy shouted. He pulled on my shirt. "Come on!"
>
> I couldn't let Linda Jean go home without those keys. I desperately swept my hands in a wide circle through the dirt

and nearly shouted with relief. I had bumped into the keys!

"I've got them!" I yelled.

Linda Jean and I scrambled to our feet and followed the others through the loose place in the fence.

"I don't think they saw us!" Tommy whispered.

"We'd better hurry home," Jimmy gasped.

"Thanks for getting me out," Leroy said, and they ran off as fast as they could.

I tossed the keys to Linda Jean, who looked scared. She grabbed them and smiled her thanks.

I could hear the doors of the police car slam, and a voice said, "I'll check inside. You take a look on the other side of that fence."

The steps came closer, and I stiffened. What that policeman would find on the other side of the fence would be Linda Jean and me!

Authors in control

Sometimes, there is a great deal a character must say, and the author has the problem of keeping this lengthy piece of dialogue from sounding like a long, boring speech.

The solution to the problem is actually easy. Authors have the power to interrupt their characters whenever they feel like it, stopping their conversations to show them—or other characters—in motion. While characters are speaking, they are moving, and it's up to authors to show this to their readers. Dialogue that is not interspersed with action and touches of description would be dull to read, no matter how interesting the conversation might be.

Other characters can interrupt the long speeches with questions or opinions of their own; the author can interrupt with short bits of narration; and the speaker can even interrupt himself with his own thoughts.

In *The Mystery of the Secret Stowaway*, Joe Riley has to tell what he knows in order to solve the mystery. If I had put it in one long paragraph, it would have been boring, so I wrote it like this, interrupting Joe often:

Everybody was looking at me as though I was crazy, and I had to talk fast.

"Remember that nothing is supposed to be missing except the clothes Mr. Riggle wore?"

"That's right. He was wearing them when he disappeared."

"No," I said. "Because Mr. Riggle didn't disappear. Miss Stanhope did."

"I think the kid is going batty," Jerry said.

"Please listen," I told them. "Miss Stanhope is missing, because there never was a Miss Stanhope. I was on the gangplank when I heard Mr. Riggle telling the officer that Miss Stanhope was already on board, even though she hadn't been checked off the list of passengers."

I took another deep breath. "Mr. Riggle just pretended there was a Miss Stanhope and paid for two staterooms. Then, the first night out, he threw that brown suit and shoes overboard, shaved off his beard, and became Miss Stanhope."

Slang and dialect

Since the life of a novel for children may be very long, authors of contemporary juvenile mysteries should not date a book with current slang. Simple, timeless expressions should generally be used. To play it safe, authors may even invent a slang word or expression if they feel slang is essential at any point.

On the other hand, using regional speech patterns to create atmosphere, authenticity, and perhaps even a "time period" in mystery novels with historical settings can help a novel ring true. Dennis Hamley's *Pageants of Despair* illustrates this point:

> ... They beckoned him to join them—and suddenly Peter felt totally scared. He was about to meet the first fifteenth-century people who had no idea who he was or where he came from. He was comforted when he had looked at them for a moment or two and had taken in their brownish smocks and stockings, their fair hair and clear skins, to realize they were

children—a boy a few years older than himself, a girl a year or two younger.

"Who art thou, then?" said the boy as Peter scrambled up the raked seats. "Thou'art not from around here. Where's thi come from?"

Peter could just make out what he said. Uncle Tom and Auntie Elsie had West Riding accents—but nothing like this.

"What's thi name?" said the girl.

"Peter," said Peter, trying hard to remember the cover story Gilbert had given him. [He tells them in a rush of words.]

"Happen tha'd better start again," said the boy.

Peter did so, and spoke very slowly. The boy and the girl listened with exaggerated care.

"From the south, tha says?" said the boy. "An actor? Tha'll be acting here, then."

"I don't know," said Peter.

"Thou shall have to change thi tooth," said the girl.

"I'll have to what?"

"Talk like us," said the boy. "I'm Francis."

In dealing with foreign accents or regional accents, it's better not to try to write the sounds literally, because it makes them too difficult to read. A few words, a change in sentence structure, as in the above example, give the feeling, which is all that is needed. In the following excerpt from *Tales of Terror,* by Ida Chittum, the flavor of the Ozark Mountains is given through the use of regional words and speech patterns, without any awkward changes in spelling to try to recreate sounds:

Mama reared up out of the covers a time or two. She thought she heard something creeping.

"There's something walking around out there amongst the dead, Papa," Mama said. "I do fear it may be Uncle Ned."

"Uncle Ned wasn't one to wear hisself out pacin' about in his lifetime. I reckon he ain't likely to take it up after death," Papa said. He grunted and rolled over and went back to sleep.

Writers may sometimes think it better to use "he cried," or "she shouted," or "he whispered," instead of "he said," but there's nothing wrong with "said" most of the time. Though it is repetitive, readers are used to seeing it, and it is less noticeable than the substitute words. If it's obvious to the readers which character is speaking, identification of the speaker is unnecessary and can be omitted.

In writing dialogue, the format calls for beginning a new paragraph each time a different character speaks, so speeches are separated and easily identifiable. Commas and periods should be put inside the quotation marks:

> "I'm going home, Jack," Sally said.

If the sentence is broken by words of identification or description, then it is written like this:

> "Jack," Sally said, looking nervously at the house, "I'm going home."

6

Description and Sensory Perception

WHAT DO authors want to achieve with description? The answer is a multiple one. They want to present a picture readers can visualize—a vivid concept, an imaginative depiction of the story that is taking place.

The primary elements of the juvenile mystery novel are the character with his problem and mystery to solve, the plot and its action. But details and description are essential, too. They make the problem seem real, the character alive, and the plot happen. Readers want to see where the action takes place, what the characters look like, and to follow in their imaginations what the main character does and where he goes.

How much detail?

This doesn't mean an author should use so many details that they detract from the story. Long pages of detailed description interfere with the action. Readers want just enough description to get a feeling for the characters, surroundings, and mood. Extraneous bits of description can be left out. There is no need to mention the weather, for example, unless it plays a part in the story. An entire house doesn't need to be described, just enough of it for readers to tell quickly whether it's a modern suburban home or a rambling Victorian mansion—whatever the author wants readers to see. A reader's imagination will fill in the gaps to create a whole picture, leaving the author to go on with the plot of the mystery.

Some things need to be detailed specifically, however, since readers in various parts of the United States, used to their own local backgrounds, see things in different ways. For example, when I was writing *Delbert, the Plainclothes Detective,* I had my main character living in a low-income section of Houston, and this meant small, wooden, single-story dwellings. However, when my editor in New York read of poverty areas, she immediately thought of multi-storied tenement buildings, but with the limited amount of description I had given, she was unable to visualize Delbert's house. Much more detail was needed.

In *The View From the Cherry Tree,* Willo Davis Roberts describes Old Lady Calloway's living room briefly, but the description of the room shows us what kind of person the woman was. The main character, Rob, has already mentioned seeing into the room through the heavy lace curtains:

> Mrs. Calloway's rug was dark red, which ought to have been pretty, but it wasn't. He couldn't tell if it was dusty, but he imagined it smelled funny, the way the old lady herself did. The furniture was all old and funny looking too, very dark and depressing.

However, detailed description of a place or an object that is the focal point in a story can be used for added emphasis. In Scott Corbett's *The Red Room Riddle,* even the title is tied to the climax of the story, in which two young boys are tricked into a terrifying room from which they must escape.

As they enter the room, not knowing that "Jamie" will trap them there, the room is described in detail, as seen through their eyes:

> Everything in the large bedroom was some shade of red. None of it was light red, either. Mostly it was a dark, blood red, from the wallpaper and the close-drawn drapes to the canopy hanging around the tall, four-poster bed. An upholstered arm-chair was covered with scarlet stain. A scarlet runner lay across the top of a red dressing table. A picture frame was trimmed with scarlet velvet, and the picture . . . Even across the room I could see what it was. It was an engraving of the same subject as the tapestry beside the staircase. The Slaughter of the Innocents. Jamie walked in and set the lamp down on the dressing table. When I hesitated on the threshold, Bill nudged me forward and followed me in. Jamie looked up at the ceiling with chuckling satisfaction. Even the ceiling was painted blood red, but it was shiny and sticky-looking, as if the paint had never dried properly.

The description of the room continues, interspersed with the boys' conversation, as Jamie tells them there is a secret stairway leading from the fireplace, and they must find it. The terror in this room begins to mount when Jamie leaves, locking the boys in, and they recognize the fact that they had better find the secret stairway and get out fast, before something dreadful happens.

Setting a mood

Description can help to create a mood. It can set the scene for humor, sorrow, or even fear and violence, as in *The Red Room Riddle.*

Description of the setting or background for any juvenile mystery novel should be interesting. It can often subtly teach the reader something about a new and different locale, giving added dimension to the story. An editor of juvenile books said recently, "I look for fiction that is interesting and exciting and that also includes a learning situation." There is no reason for a mystery not to offer this learning situation, too, and the setting of the story is often the means to achieve this.

Sometimes, the location can be an exotic one. *Meet Me at Tamerlane's Tomb,* by Barbara Corcoran, takes place in Samarkand and involves crime in the USSR. And *Cat in the Mirror,* by Mary Stolz, takes its main character back to ancient Egypt. Both settings are unfamiliar to many young readers, and a great deal of detailed description is needed to make these settings come alive, thus conveying to the reader something new about these places. Writers who want to emphasize setting as an integral part of their novels or stories should, whenever possible, learn their locations first-hand by visiting them and studying them. They should meet the people who inhabit the areas, as well as read everything they can find about them. If, however, the setting plays only a minimal part in the story, requiring only light touches of atmosphere, then writers can use travel articles, maps, street guides for walking tours, time tables, brochures from the chamber of commerce, books—anything that deals with the particular place that is to be used as the setting—to provide the background and necessary description.

Locales in the United States that are familiar to a writer can be just as exciting as faraway places. In my mystery novel, *The Mysterious Red Tape Gang,* I used a typical neighborhood in Los Angeles—an area close to the one where I had grown up. I included a schoolroom setting in many of the chapters, because an editor once said to me, "We get so many, many mysteries which take place during summer vacation. Why can't writers occasionally include a familiar school setting in their stories? Children can easily relate to the classroom."

A nearby locale, which seems too familiar to be exciting to a writer, can be unusual and fascinating to children in other parts of the United States and to children in other countries who read our mysteries translated into their own languages.

The five senses—touch, taste, smell, sound, and sight—play an integral part in description. Authors can help their readers see life with the same excitement and clarity as they see it by making full use of sensory perception. Stories become more real to readers when they use their five senses in reading, thus becoming more involved.

In *The Secret of the Elms*, by Daniel P. Mannix, readers share Mary Ellen's sense of hearing, touch, and sight in this scene:

> It was still night when she awakened suddenly. The candle had burned itself out and she could barely make out the outlines of the windows; everything else was in complete blackness. Something had awakened her, but she knew not what.
>
> Then she heard footsteps coming up the stairs. They were light steps, but distinct. She lay motionless, rigid with terror. Perhaps whatever it was would not know she was here. The door creaked slightly. Something had come into the room and was going toward the closet. Mary Ellen could stand no more.
>
> "Who are you?" she screamed. Instantly the steps stopped while Mary Ellen felt the goose flesh spring out, and her stomach turned over with fear. She wanted to move but was paralyzed.
>
> She heard the steps coming toward her bed. She opened her mouth to cry out, but no sound came. Something was standing by the bed looking at her. In spite of the darkness, she was conscious of a white oval face with keen eyes like her grandmother's studying her. A cold breeze seemed to come from the apparition and blow across her, a coldness of a sort she had never known. Then the breeze stopped and she knew she was alone in the room.

While the senses of taste and smell are not used as frequently in fiction as the other three senses, they still serve the purpose of drawing readers into the story, calling upon their imaginations to share an experience. In *The Mysterious Red Tape Gang,* I wanted to cause a rift between the boys in the club and Linda Jean. Describing the situation through sensory perception helped the reader participate:

> "Okay," I said. "What's that horrible smell?"
>
> "What horrible smell?" Linda Jean asked, so we knew it had to be her.
>
> "Something smells all sweet and sticky and spoiled and rotten," I told her.
>
> She sniffed and looked insulted. "Well, because you are boys, you don't recognize perfume when you smell it. It happens to be a very lovely perfume."
>
> "My mother wears perfume," Leroy said, "and she sure doesn't smell like that!"
>
> "Well, I decided I want to be a chemist when I grow up, so I made my perfume myself. I read about it in a book, and you're supposed to use rose petals, except we don't have any rose bushes, so I used some petunias and marigolds and dandelions instead."
>
> "We have a rule in this club," I told her, "that nobody can wear perfume to club meetings."
>
> "Hah!" she said. "When did you make up a rule like that?"
>
> "Like right now," I said. "Furthermore, anybody who happens to wear perfume, not knowing about the rule, has to sit outside the door, so the other people in the club won't get sick to their stomachs."

Clichés and figures of speech

In writing passages of description, you may find that you have put in a cliché or two, since we all are so accustomed to hearing them in our everyday conversation. Reading your manuscript aloud can help you catch and eliminate some of these too-familiar phrases that may have crept in.

Writers must always look for original ways to express ideas, and using similes and metaphors in describing the setting of the mystery is often an effective technique. For example, in a mystery novel taking place at the ocean, anything related to the sea can be utilized:

> When I heard the sound behind me, my back felt all prickly
> and scratchy, as though one of those little sand crabs was scut-
> tling up and down my spine.

Or . . .

> Hiding in that rowboat. Laura was just as tense as the line
> that tied it to the pier, with the tide tugging and tugging at the
> boat, trying to move it out to sea.

Most writers would come up with the automatic answer
of "adjectives and adverbs" when asked to think of words
that describe. Yet when a word is needed for vivid description that will grab the reader's attention, an action verb is
often best for the job. One verb can present a complete
picture, telling readers in an instant what they should know.
Suppose a character is about to leave the room. Readers can
see him more clearly if they are told that he *shuffles* or
stomps or *dashes,* or even *stumbles* from the room. Each of
these verbs not only shows exactly what the character is
doing, but many of them express a hidden emotion. Perhaps
the boy who stumbles from the room is so frightened or
nervous that he can't manage to get out any other way. The
man who stomps must be very angry, or he would certainly
remember to control his actions.

Notice the mental picture drawn up by these verbs from
Through a Brief Darkness, by Richard Peck:

> Blanche lost her head completely, whirled and darted for the
> open deck. The stewards broke rank and jammed through the
> door after her. And the curious passengers surged after them.

And these from *The Case of the Condemned Cat,* by
E. W. Hildick:

But he didn't get any further, because that's when McGurk put his idea into action. Already he'd taken out the mint wrapper. He was fiddling with it, seemingly nervous, not knowing what he was doing. Just smoothing it out, then twisting it and untwisting it. And crossing and uncrossing his fingers at the same time.

And these, from *The Mystery of Hurricane Castle:*

The wind tore at their clothing and pushed against them, scratching their arms and legs with bits of flying sea shells and rocks.

In a juvenile mystery novel, the action is usually more intense and the pace of the story quicker than in any other type of writing for children. For this reason, most mystery writers find it essential to break up their descriptive passages and blend the description with the action and dialogue—particularly toward the climax of the story, when the pace and action quicken even more.

Young readers, excitedly living with the main character through each suspense-filled chapter, will not stop to analyze how they have become involved completely in the story. The point is that they *are* involved; and skillful, subtle use of description helps achieve this goal.

7

Great Beginnings
and Satisfying Endings

IN THE JUVENILE mystery, especially, children want to be flung into the action. The opening sentences must grab their attention so they will keep reading.

Editors' decisions are often based on the opening of the story—how well it is written, how it catches the reader's attention, how it involves the main character of the story. Editors know that the children for whom they are publishing are even more critical than they are. Children don't have the compulsion that adults have to finish a book, once they've begun it. They read the opening paragraphs—or maybe only sentences—of a story, and decide then and there whether to finish reading the book or to toss it down and look for one they'd enjoy more.

How to start a story

In *Here Lies the Body,* by Scott Corbett, the story opening utilizes the technique of including a word children would immediately think of as "scary," so they will want to read on to see if they are going to be as frightened as they hope they will be:

> Everything we experienced, many long years ago, happened to us because my brother Mitch got a summer job mowing grass in a cemetery.

In the opening sentence of *The Ghost Belonged to Me*, Richard Peck makes a straightforward, frightening statement that challenges the reader to go further into the story:

> At one time there was a ghost out in the brick barn on the back of our place.

Sebastian, Super Sleuth, by Mary Blount Christian, opens with fast-paced physical action:

> The door marked Police Chief burst open and the scowling, beetle-browed chief stormed into the small waiting room.
> "Get in here, Detective John Quincy Jones! On the double! Quick!"

Fear is the emotion felt by the main character in *Z for Zachariah* (Robert C. O'Brien). The suspense is heightened when the readers are not told right away why the character is afraid, and they must continue reading in order to find out:

> May 20.
> I am afraid.
> Someone is coming.
> That is, I think someone is coming, though I am not sure, and I pray that I am wrong.

The opening in *The View from the Cherry Tree* is a quieter one, yet the reader can tell that it sets the scene for trouble to come:

> From his perch in the cherry tree Rob Mallory could see into
> the houses on either side. It was the Mallorys' tree, but it was
> closest to Mrs. Calloway's house; right up against it, as a matter
> of fact, and one of the numerous causes of problems with their
> neighbor.

The beginning sentence of a story should be so arresting that it will attract the reader's attention immediately. Sometimes it will come on with a bang; other times it will be low key and full of the suspenseful mood the writer wants to express. The opening of the book can even be humorous, if a humorous tone is to be continued throughout the mystery novel. But in any case, it should set in motion the action of the story.

For example, Willo Davis Roberts could have begun the story in *The View from the Cherry Tree* by describing the turmoil in the Mallory household as Rob's big sister is preparing to get married. She could have told us about the family and their frantic plans, and Rob's feelings of being left out and ignored, as all the attention centered on his sister. But the author saved these pieces of information to use later in her novel, knowing that readers wouldn't be interested in details until after they had been drawn into the story and were excitedly reading to see what would happen to Rob.

Since the cherry tree plays a prominent part in the story, even in the murder of Old Lady Calloway, the author includes it in the beginning sentence, placing it firmly in the minds of the readers.

The early paragraphs of a story, following the strong opening sentence, should present the mystery, or a hint of the mystery to come, or set the stage so that the reader knows something exciting is going to happen. These paragraphs should introduce the main character and any important minor characters, and arouse the reader's emotional reactions to the story. If the mystery is going to involve deductive reasoning, or make the reader laugh, or be frightened, the reader has a right to know that from the very beginning.

Five questions

The journalistic five questions are answered in the first paragraphs of the juvenile mystery novel: *Who* is involved in the mystery? *What* is happening to him? *When* and *where* is this story taking place? And *why* did the whole thing come about?

When I wrote the opening for *The Mystery of the Secret Stowaway,* there was quite a bit of information I wanted to impart right off. The *who* was my main character, Joe Riley. The *what* was the situation in which he found himself: the predicament of Mrs. Crumbacher's getting angry with him, which led to his involvement with the luxury liner and the mystery on board. The *when* and *where* would be the setting in a modern house in a residential Los Angeles neighborhood. And the *why* was the reason Joe was in trouble. I needed to give some of his background, and yet start the story with some action that would catch the reader's attention immediately. The opening of the story came out like this:

> I always seem to be in trouble, and it's never my fault. Well, most of the time it isn't. It certainly wasn't my fault when Mrs. Crumbacher got so mad at me.
>
> "Joe Riley!" she kept yelling. "You are the worst eleven-year-old troublemaker I've ever laid eyes on!"
>
> And all I had been trying to do was make someone happy.
>
> Mrs. Crumbacher is the lady I live with when my dad is away on location with a movie crew. He's a technician, which means that he helps to move cameras and furniture and scenery used on movie sets, and all sorts of things like that. It's a real neat job, and he says he meets lots of crazy people and lots of nice people. The only trouble is that he has to go away for months at

a time when the company is making movies in another place besides in Los Angeles, where we live.

The story then goes into the *why* and into the mystery itself. Readers are not shown right away what has happened to make Mrs. Crumbacher so angry, and by the time they find out—in the first chapter—they are well into the adventure of the mystery with Joe and involved in wondering what is going to happen to him next.

The personal problem that the main character has to face and solve should come near the beginning of the story, too, and it should be brought out in a sympathetic way, so that readers will become emotionally involved.

The problem is usually presented *before* the mystery and leads the reader into it, as in *The Mystery of the Hidden Cockatoo.* Pam Peters, on a visit to her aunt in New Orleans, thinks:

> This was where she belonged—in a city of mystery and excitement.
> At home her brothers and sisters would have laughed at that idea. They thought of her as just the oldest, the thirteen-year-old sister who shouldn't mind a bit when one of them lost her new, colored pencils, or teased her about being too plump, or borrowed her best nightgown for a slumber party and spilled cocoa down the front of the lace ruffles . . .

However, in some juvenile mysteries, particularly the detective type, the mystery itself comes first, then the personal problem. In *The Case of the Condemned Cat,* a "client" comes to the McGurk firm of private investigators to ask them to take on a case in which his cat is accused of killing a neighbor's dove. As the story develops, the problem develops too: the boy's fear that his cat will be taken away from him; and his unsympathetic mother, who is insistent that they get rid of the cat, without trying to find out if the cat is really the culprit.

Endings with hope—and logic

Everything in the juvenile mystery novel should be logical and believable to the reader, especially the ending. The ending doesn't have to be a happy one. In fact, in some cases it is better not to have a happy ending, because under certain circumstances, a happy ending would not be either logical or believable.

In *Z for Zachariah,* Ann, the main character, in order to save her life, manages to take John Loomis's safe suit, and leaves John and the valley that has sheltered her. She goes out into the world that had been devastated by a nuclear war, wondering what lies ahead. The last paragraph in the book is this:

> Now it is morning. I do not know where I am. I walked all afternoon and almost all night until I was so tired I could not go on. Then I did not bother to put up the tent, just spread my blanket by the roadside and lay down. While I was sleeping the dream came, and in the dream I walked until I found the school-room and the children. When I awoke, the sun was high in the sky. A stream was flowing through the brown grass, winding west. The dream was gone, yet I knew which way to go. As I walk I search the horizon for a trace of green. I am hopeful.

In *The Mystery of the Secret Stowaway,* Joe Riley could not be allowed to get off scot-free from his adventure as a stowaway, even though he hadn't stowed away on the ship deliberately. The grateful Dodi has given him Feef, the poodle, as a goodbye present, when Joe's father comes to the ship to get his son. As Joe and his father drive away in a taxi, the book ends on this note:

> I knew that whenever we got to Dad's hotel room, there was going to be the dickens to pay, but oh, well . . . I had Feef, hadn't I?
>
> I rubbed my chin up and down her curly head, promising

myself that in the future I would do just the things that grown-
ups wanted me to do, and wondering how I was ever going to
manage to stay out of trouble.

Both endings—in spite of their implications of future
problems for the main characters—offer the element of
hope, which I feel should be an essential ingredient in any
children's story. Young people have not had the experience
to handle problems that seem to have no solutions, and they
don't need to close a book with a feeling of despair.

There is no place for coincidence in a mystery story,
either in the solution of the character's problem or the solution of the mystery. It's up to the authors to use their
imaginations to get their characters out of tight spots. The
it-was-all-a-dream solution is in the same category as the
coincidence. It makes readers—who have been rooting for
the main character throughout the book, wondering how he
or she will use wit and daring to reach the solution—feel as
though the author has played a dirty trick. The main character must solve the problem, no matter how difficult a
problem the author has set up.

To keep from writing your main characters into the kind
of trap from which you can't imagine how to extricate
them, think first of the main character and the mystery and
the personal problem to be tackled. Next think of how the
main character can reach his solution as described earlier.
Once the beginning and the end of the mystery novel are
worked out, the middle will more easily fall into place.
While it is possible for a writer simply to sit down at a
typewriter and work on a book-length manuscript, not
knowing in what direction the story will go next, in the
mystery story it's of great importance to know how all the
pieces of the story will fit together and how it will reach its
proper ending.

The mystery should end soon after the climax of the plot

has been reached. The "drawing room" type of ending, in which the detective assembles all the suspects and, after a recap of the crime, points to the one who committed it, has gone out of style even in most adult novels. Young readers want action throughout their mystery novels, and they won't hold still for this old-fashioned type of ending. The clues in the mystery should be arranged so that when the crime is solved or the villain captured, readers can say, "Of course. I should have known that was the way it would end."

Loose ends should be tied up in the last few pages of the mystery novel. Characters—even minor ones—should not be left dangling. Readers should feel satisfied with the way the plot worked out and the way the characters were handled.

Arnold Madison maintains suspense in *The Secret of the Carved Whale Bone* right into the ending, when Pete thinks he has discovered the "treasure" and saved his uncle's fishing business. As everyone crowds around to see the emerald Pete has uncovered, they find out from a jeweler that it's only green glass. Suddenly, the situation is even more hopeless than it was before. With just four pages to go to the end of the book, Pete realizes where the real emerald has been hidden. The mystery is solved just three paragraphs from the end of this suspenseful novel. And the last piece falls neatly into place, with the personal problem taken care of and all the clues and "plants" accounted for. It presents an excellent example of ending a book when it should end, without one unnecessary word stretching out the story beyond the climax.

Climaxes

The climax is one of the most important scenes in the mystery novel. The entire story has been leading up to this scene. The situation has been made to look nearly impossible for the main character. Maybe, like Rob in *The*

View from the Cherry Tree, the main character's life is in danger; or, like Ann in *Z for Zachariah,* she is in a predicament that seems to be hopeless. However, because of the decisions these main characters make, the actions they take, they are able to face the danger and win.

Beginning writers often tend to skip over the climax scene too quickly, telling in a few words what happened, and reassuring their readers that it turned out all right for their main characters. It's essential to *show* this scene taking place, not simply to tell about it, so that readers can participate in it. Everything at the author's command—dialogue, sensory perception, description, action—all the techniques that make for good writing should be utilized in writing the climax of the juvenile mystery.

Techniques That Work

IN WRITING juvenile mystery novels, especially for readers from the ages of eight to twelve, it's most effective to tell the story from the viewpoint of one character only. Although some books have been published which break this rule, it is still difficult for children, as they read fiction, to jump from the mind of one character to another. They would rather relate to the main character and follow him or her all the way to the end.

Viewpoint characters: readers' guides

It's up to the writer to decide just who is going to take the reader through the novel. The best way to do this is to pick the character closest to the problem. A story is stronger when the action is happening to the main character. It is less interesting if it is presented through the eyes of a less important character.

In most juvenile mysteries, moreover, the author wants the reader to feel the same emotions as the main character—especially fear—and this can be done most easily by presenting the story from inside the mind of the main character. In

The Secret of the Elms, Daniel P. Mannix has set up a situation in which three cousins come to visit their grandmother—each instructed by her parents how to act so she'll be chosen as heiress to the grandmother's estate. The three girls, who have never met before, are different types. The author has chosen Mary Ellen as the one to whom readers would find it easiest to relate, and the story is presented from her point of view. So it is Mary Ellen who has the encounters with the ghost, Mary Ellen who defies her grandmother when she thinks the old woman is wrong, and Mary Ellen who takes the initiative in convincing her grandmother that she should recognize the existence of her only grandson. Presented through the eyes of this one girl, the novel has more dramatic impact than if it were divided in viewpoint.

When novelists write from the viewpoint of a single character, they must not reveal any knowledge of events or people which that viewpoint character does not yet have. The main character can tell, of course, if another character has been crying or upset. Authors don't have to switch viewpoint to inform their readers what the observed character is doing or how she is reacting. The viewpoint character can see things, think about them, and even guess what is in the minds of other characters. On occasion, this guesswork can be used to accentuate the problem or conflict in the story.

In Phyllis A. Whitney's *Secret of Haunted Mesa,* Jenny, the main character, is unable to understand her older sister, who, while still in her teens, is a famous singer. Because of this lack of understanding, Jenny's problems are intensified. Near the end of the mystery novel, this conversation takes place between the two sisters, as Jenny tells Carol she wouldn't miss college for anything:

"But you don't have anything else you want to do," Carol pointed out.

For the first time, Jenny found that she didn't altogether accept this. "Oh, I expect there'll be lots of things I'll want to do."

Carol looked at her, puzzled. "You sound different. I mean different since we came here."

Jenny thought about this. She didn't feel any different. "I don't know what you mean."

"You've stopped being jealous of me," Carol said with unexpected understanding. "You never needed to be, you know. You're clever in lots of ways I'm not. I've just got one thing I can do well. It's the only way I know to make people pay attention to me."

Jenny stared at her in surprise. She hadn't thought Carol had noticed that much.

The novel of deduction, however, is sometimes an exception; here, if the main character is an unusual person with idiosyncrasies and eccentricities—or even superhuman mental powers—the story can be told from the viewpoint of a minor character. By this means, the minor character can point out the unusual, even strange, characteristics of the main character, a method that could not be used if the novel were written from the viewpoint of the main character.

This Watson-Sherlock Holmes technique in the juvenile novel is exemplified by the McGurk mystery series by E. W. Hildick, in which Joey, as secretary of McGurk's detective club, tells the story in first person, often pointing out McGurk's special talents in solving crimes.

First person versus third person

A story for young people can be told in either first person or third person. Which to use is often determined by which comes more naturally to the author. There was a time when juvenile fiction written in the first person was discouraged by editors, but now many books in the first person are being published. Sometimes it's easier for a beginning writer to compose his story in first person, because it eliminates the danger of getting mixed up in multiple viewpoint, with other characters' thoughts coming into the story unbidden, and confusing the reader. And sometimes first person simply "feels right" to the author.

In the first-person viewpoint, the story is told from the position of "I." The action will be happening to the person telling the story. The author must be careful not to make "I" a conceited super-person. "I" will be frank with the reader about his inner feelings—how scared he gets, how mixed up he can be at times. He must be open about his thoughts as well as his actions. The author should be careful not to let "I" simply tell *about* the story. All the action must be shown, complete with dialogue, as in this example from *The Mystery of the Secret Stowaway:*

> I went on eating, and for a long time Harriet was quiet, which was a real miracle. I finished the last bite and put down my fork.
> "Do you understand grownups?" I asked her.
> "No," she said. "Why?"
> "They do the darndest things. Here Dodi Doll was hiding something real and insisting it was missing when it wasn't, and Miss Stanhope is insisting nothing is missing when something is."
> "What is?" she asked.
> "Whatever was in the package."
> A shadow fell across the newspaper, and I looked up to see Miss Stanhope going past us. She didn't pause, but she looked at me with pure hatred in her eyes. It was such an awful look that it scared me. Why should she stare at me like that? Had she overheard what I'd said about the package?

Most juvenile mystery stories are written in the third person. Again, the character closest to the problem is picked, given a name, and the story is told from his or her single viewpoint, as in this example from *Mystery of the Grinning Idol:*

> Eileen let out a screech, jumped up and tore through the bushes, racing toward the path. The full skirt swished around her legs, feeling like a strange thing clawing at her, pulling her back. She was sure that she heard footsteps following rapidly behind her, and she nearly sobbed. He must not catch her! He mustn't!
>
> Past the dark swimming pool, through the shadowy paths she ran, gasping for breath, her legs aching. The footsteps clattered behind her. Whoever he was, he was coming nearer!
>
> Then, all of a sudden, a path of light streamed out across the darkness. Mrs. Medina was standing in the open doorway. Eileen rushed up to her, panting for breath.
>
> "He's right behind me!" she managed to gasp. "Help!"

Transitions

The unimportant things that characters do can be taken care of through transitions, which are bridges from one scene to another. Transitions can be very short or very long, depending upon how much material needs to be covered in them. Here are some short ones:

> After she washed the dishes, Penny went back to the living room and said to her sister . . .
>
> The next morning . . .
>
> When he arrived at school . . .
>
> Three days later he still felt the same way about the old house. He phoned Bob and said . . .

Short transitions are used when the reader does not need to know details, or to be filled in on the emotional state of the main character or what he or she did or thought during the skipped-over period of time.

Long transitions can take a paragraph or more, and will explain the actions or emotions of the character, perhaps, or give information the reader should know before moving on to the next scene. For example, in *The Mysterious Red Tape Gang,* as a scene ends, we move into this transition:

> I knew I should say something to comfort her, but I couldn't very well say, "Don't feel bad because your father is a criminal," or "Let's just keep hoping he doesn't go to prison." And I couldn't think of anything else.
>
> She walked off, holding her shoulders back and head straight, but I had the feeling she was crying again.
>
> Mom and Dad took Terry and me to a movie that afternoon. It was supposed to be a comedy, but I couldn't get my mind off Mr. Hartwell and didn't feel much like laughing.
>
> It seemed forever until we had come home, eaten dinner, and it began to get dark . . .

And on into the next scene.

Realism for young readers

Mystery stories for readers from eight to twelve aren't usually gory or horrifying. Characters can be captured or threatened, but description should be kept within the bounds of good sense and taste. Readers of mystery novels want to be frightened, but authors should not go so far that they give these young people nightmares!

There was a time in which no dead bodies were written into stories for this age group, but lately this situation has changed. Although death is found in the juvenile mystery, it is still used sparingly. In *The View from the Cherry Tree,* eleven-year-old Rob does witness the death of Old Lady Calloway, and it is described as it happens. But in *Here Lies the Body,* the boys hear the sounds of old Ezekiel being murdered, and come into the house after the deed has been done. They see only his legs and the symbol of witchcraft on the window, and they run for the police.

Here Lies the Body, which deals with witchcraft, is an

example of the unexplained occult found in many current novels for readers in the eight-to-twelve age group. Other occult subjects in recent juvenile mysteries include clairvoyance, changelings and evil fairies, preternatural forces, and even the devil himself. The unreal is now acceptable in the mystery novel for young people.

Most types of crimes can be depicted in the juvenile mystery, from shoplifting to kidnapping to dope smuggling; but violence is kept at a minimum. When a mystery story is based on a criminal act, the deduction and solution must be dealt with accurately.

Titles

A librarian once told me, "When I see the words 'mystery,' 'secret,' or 'ghost' in the title of a book for children, I automatically order five copies, because I know the books will be read so eagerly they will soon be in shreds."

If authors keep this in mind and make their titles mysterious or fearful, children who want the pleasure of traveling with a character through a scary adventure will reach for such books.

It's common in juvenile mysteries to give a short title to each chapter also. These titles should hint at some mysterious event or possible danger that will take place within the chapter. Titles should never give away secrets in the chapter, however, but serve as "teasers" to whet the readers' appetites for more mystery to come, and to create further suspense. To illustrate the point, some of the chapter titles I used in *The Mysterious Red Tape Gang* were: "The Secret Plan," "A Dangerous Mistake," "Something Strange is Going On," and "Do Something, Mike!"

Mysteries for Younger Readers

THE JUVENILE mystery has crept down into the picture book level, where it has dropped all of its frightening aspects and has become more of a curious puzzle to figure out. Pure and simple detection is the mystery technique used in the picture book mystery.

The Thump, Blam, Bump Mystery, by Louise Armstrong, is an example of this uncomplicated mystery story. Erma Jean tells it in the first person. On the first page she states:

> . . . And what I like best
> is any kind of mystery.
>
> A mystery's when something happens
> and you don't know what made it,
> or when something gets done
> but you don't know what did it.

She then proceeds to tell about her friends in the apartment house, each child living under the one on the floor above, from the ninth floor down to the third. At the top, Roger hears a noise which causes him to drop something, making a noise below, and on the situation goes. Erma Jean, on the third floor, is frightened, and goes up to the penthouse apartment with her mother and the other children in the building, to discover the cause of the original loud thump. Thus the mystery is solved.

Richard Scarry in his *Great Steamboat Mystery* takes newlyweds Mr. and Mrs. Pig to a wedding party on board a steamboat. The guests come in costume, and among them there is a jewel thief who makes away with Mrs. Pig's new pearl necklace.

Joining picture and text

Neither of these plots would be frightening to younger children, but each encourages them to use their own powers of deduction, along with the main characters in the stories. Clues are given in the text and in the pictures. The texts alone do not carry the complete mysteries with all their plants and clues. In the picture book mystery, the illustrations do their part, and authors who do not illustrate their own books should include information as to what clues ought to be illustrated. Authors should never try to instruct illustrators in how to illustrate their books—only give them pertinent facts that need to be shown in the illustrations.

Unless the author is also a professional illustrator, familiar with the various processes used in book illustration, the choice of illustrator will be left up to the editor. It's never necessary for an author to try to find an illustrator. In fact, if an editor doesn't like the illustrations that are submitted with a manuscript, he or she will be very likely to turn down the manuscript, which might have been accepted, if it had been submitted without illustrations.

Also, because authors can depend on illustrators to share in telling their stories, they do not need to use as much description of characters or places in the text as they would in a book for older children. In most cases, the illustrations can present all the physical description.

Richard Scarry (who illustrates his own books), in his *Great Steamboat Mystery,* offers a good example of illustrations showing many of the clues in the mystery. Sam and Dudley, famous detectives (a cat and a pig), are hired to protect the wedding gifts aboard the steamboat *Sally,* where the wedding guests are partying with the bride and groom, Mr. and Mrs. Pig. There are many characters in Richard Scarry's illustrations, and occasionally some of them are doing things that might be construed as suspicious. On most of the pages, readers can see part of a face peering out of a porthole, or peeking over the top of a keg on deck, or from behind a door. The person who stole Mrs. Pig's pearls while she napped in a deck chair left white powder on her dress. Dudley and Sam try to track down people who have white powder on their clothes, and the clues show up in the illustrations, so the child who cannot read the book to himself can pick up the clues from the pictures.

In Scarry's "Supermarket Mystery," from *The Great Big Mystery Book,* the observant young reader will see the clues to who is stealing groceries in the busy, funny illustrations. But the author uses a red herring by introducing (in the text) the woman with the large hat filled with "fruit," leading Dudley to jump to false conclusions.

Because of the simplicity of the plot of the picture book mystery, authors must be especially careful not to use just an incident instead of a complete plot. Even the picture book mystery story must have a beginning, a middle, and an ending, with a main character involved in solving a mystery. For this age, and because of word limitations, the personal problem is not developed as much as in books for older children, and sometimes it is omitted. However, the characters must be well rounded, believable and likable individuals, with personal traits all their own. And suspense should be maintained throughout the story, since that is the purpose of the mystery for any age group.

The length of the picture book mystery is variable. Some stories can be just a few words to a page long, with most of the action carried in the illustrations, while others can be a few thousand words. Most picture books will be under 1,500 words, so that there will be plenty of space in a 32-page book for large illustrations.

Authors should try to visualize how their manuscripts will fit into the 26 to 28 pages that will be allotted to text in a 32-page book. The typed text can be divided as if it were on separate printed pages, rather than typed as a continuous story.

Is there some piece of action which can easily be illustrated on each "page"? If not, there should be. Picture book mysteries use even more physical movement than mysteries for older readers; illustrations, then, can be varied and intriguing.

The final version of a manuscript may be typed in "pages," that is, divided as the author envisages it will be broken up in the printed book. For such a typed version, use about eight spaces between the separate "pages." Several such "pages" will fit onto one sheet of typewriter paper. While it is not necessary to type the manuscript this way, indicating how the author thinks it will be divided when in published form, it does give editors the overall view the author has for the set-up of the book.

Many picture book mysteries are humorous as well as suspenseful. This humor should be interesting to the child and to the adult who is reading the book aloud. It's tempting at times to include something that will seem clever to another adult but will be over the head of the young child. Keep in mind that it is a child's book, and everything in it should be aimed at the child's level of understanding.

For beginning readers

With the increase in the last few years in books for beginning readers, ages six to eight and in the first three grades, it is natural that the popular mystery should move into that age level. Books brought out for beginning readers by a textbook house usually have a controlled vocabulary, and the authors must write to a rigid word list supplied by the publishers for a particular grade. Books published by trade publishers for beginning readers, however, are not usually limited to a specified word list or vocabulary. The trade book editors expect authors to use common sense in choosing words that are familiar to young readers.

Words must be fairly simple, or easy enough for the child to figure out in the context of the sentence. Sentences must be kept short.

The writer who is not sure of the reading vocabulary acceptable for the first three grades can visit a local elementary school and study the books used in the classroom.

The format of a mystery for beginning readers varies from publisher to publisher, and authors should study books in this category brought out by the particular publishers to whom they wish to submit material. Some of these will have as few as 550 words in a 48-page book; others are much longer. As in the presentation of picture books, authors of mysteries for beginning readers should give the illustrator ample opportunity for pictures with exciting and lively action.

Basically, authors of beginning mysteries can set a pattern for themselves. A 48-page book will mean about 40 to 43 pages of text. A 64-page book will require about 56 to 59 pages of text. These are the two most common lengths for the beginning reader books. Because of the larger print used in these books, authors should limit themselves to under 38 letters to a line, which means usually no more than eight words. Twelve lines per printed page should be maximum, and there should be very few pages this long, because on a 12-line page there will be no room for illustrations. Most pages average four to six lines to a page.

Authors may type the final version of beginning mysteries in this format (similar to that used for the picture book mystery), and leave eight spaces between each "page," making sure each one is numbered. Again, it is a good idea to include in the text for each "page" a suggested action that can be visually expressed by the artist in the illustrations.

For example, I typed the first three pages of *The Secret Box Mystery* on one sheet of typewriter paper like this:

(Page 1)
Michael John carried his box carefully
as he walked to school.
It was a shoe box.

(Page 2)
But it did not have shoes in it.
There were two small holes in one end.
And what was in the box was
Michael John's secret.

(Page 3)
As he came to the corner,
Wilma ran out of her house.
She didn't say, "Hello."
She said, "What's in the box?"
Wilma was like that.

These opening pages also illustrate the fact that the main character and the mystery are brought out in the very beginning of the story. Wilma is an important minor character, involved in the mystery, so she is quickly brought in, too, and her character established in just a few words. With this beginning mystery format, the writer is challenged to give a great deal of information in the fewest number of words possible.

My book *The Mysterious Prowler* opens with the introduction of the main character and action:

> "There is a shadow on the porch,"
> Jonathan said.
> "I think someone is looking in our
> window!"
>
> He ran to the window, but the
> shadow was gone.
> He opened the door, but no one was
> on the porch.

In the story, someone leaves a noseprint on Jonathan's window and bicycle tracks across his muddy yard, then calls on the phone but does not speak. Jonathan sets out to discover who the prowler is. As in the eight-to-twelve novel, the solution of this beginning mystery is in the hands of the main character, although he is allowed to have a little more help from his friends.

Crosby N. Bonsall has created an enchanting group of clubhouse characters who people a number of her beginning reader books. Wizard, Tubby, Skinny and Snitch solve simple mysteries. In *The Case of the Hungry Stranger,* they try to discover who stole a neighbor's blueberry pie. In *The Case of the Cat's Meow,* author Bonsall has them search for Snitch's missing cat. And in *The Case of the Scaredy Cats,* a group of neighborhood girls try to take over the boys' clubhouse. When, after a fight in the snow, one of the littlest girls is missing, the boy detectives hunt for her—and succeed in their search. Each of these books has an uncomplicated plot, with a question to be answered, a problem to be solved. The early attempts to solve the mystery fail, building suspense before the final attempt succeeds.

In Mary Blount Christian's *Goosehill Gang* series, simple mystery plots are used, but with a difference. Published by a religious publishing house, each mystery—with its personal problem to be solved—hinges on a Bible verse. For example, in *The Goosehill Gang and the Vanishing Sandwich*, Beth proves the message of the Good Samaritan—"go and do likewise"—by discovering the reason for the mysterious, aloof behavior of Marigold during lunch period. When she sees that Marigold has been bringing an empty lunchbox to school, she and the gang, with the help of Beth's mother, remedy the situation.

The series mystery is popular in the beginning reader format. *Nate, the Great,* by Marjorie W. Sharmat, is a favorite series character who is something of a young Sam Spade. The author has picked Spade's terse detective style to add extra humor to the plots, as Nate, the Great, goes about solving crimes for his friends.

Anthropomorphism

Animal characters who behave and speak like people— called anthropomorphism—are rarely found in mystery novels for the eight-to-twelve age group, but are popular in mysteries for younger readers. When animals are the main characters in such stories, they take on human qualities, behaving much as people would do in the same situations. But though it is permissible for animals to speak among themselves, they should not speak to human beings. There is more leeway allowed here for a kind of exaggerated humor than in books with people as the main characters.

In *The Bear Detectives,* by Stanley and Janice Berenstain, the bear children try to discover who stole Farmer Ben's pumpkin. They succeed, in spite of the fact that their father behaves very badly, becoming quite bossy and wanting everyone to follow his lead in searching for clues, even though he is obviously heading in the wrong direction. With a human father, this situation would be too exaggerated to be believable, and the father would be an unsympathetic person. In this popular bear family, however, very young readers can accept anything, especially contrary or ludicrous behavior on the part of the father bear.

Children love the animal characters in the Richard Scarry mysteries. These characters are given human traits, the villains quite likely to be acting and reacting out of jealousy, conceit, or just plain "badness." The animals are friendly characters on the whole, and young readers can easily identify with their stories, as they try to figure out the clues.

Fear, humor, love

"Crimes" in the mystery for younger children are not usually crimes at all, but are puzzles that fit into their limited frame of reference—their small worlds, with themselves as the center; their fears (as seen in *The Thump, Blam, Bump Mystery*) of unexplained noises; or fear of the dark or of large animals. They like to read about children their own ages, or imaginary anthropomorphic characters, and these stories should have humor and love. Above all else, in the picture book and beginning reader mystery for young children, there must be happy endings.

10

Mystery Novels for Teen-Agers

THERE IS sometimes a fine line between the mystery novel for adult readers and that for the teen-age or young adult reader. Usually, the main characters in the young adult mysteries are teen-agers, or in their early twenties, although in Joan Aiken's *Died on a Rainy Sunday* the heroine is a married woman with two young children. In the young adult mystery, there are usually no graphic descriptions of gore and violence, but there can be plenty of terror; and while there is always romance, there are no explicit sex scenes.

Who are the readers of mystery novels for the young adult? Whereas books for younger children can be catalogued fairly close to age groupings, the young adult mystery is read by a broad range of readers. Junior high school students read young adult mysteries for pleasure and entertainment, as do many advanced readers in the upper elementary grades. Mysteries for teen-agers find many readers among the adult population, and more than any other area of mysteries for children, these books must be interesting to adults as well as to the age group for which they are specifically aimed—the twelve-to-sixteen-year-old readers.

In writing mystery novels for young adults, writers may have a wider scope for their characterizations, may delve more deeply into psychological aspects; the plots may be more fully developed. Also, multiple viewpoint is permissible, because for older readers there is not a need to establish rapport with only one central character.

In some cases, a story may be better when written in multiple viewpoint. One such example is *Home Is Where Your Feet Are Standing,* by Patricia Windsor, a novel which takes place in a town in England. Some odd things are happening in the house. Two people in town know that the house is haunted. One doesn't want Mrs. Daniel (the children's mother) to know, because he is hoping a romance will develop between him and Mrs. Daniel. The other wants to hurry the haunting process along because she is jealous and wants Mrs. Daniel and her children to leave. The teenage daughters don't know there's a ghost in the house, but work out "happenings" themselves, hoping their mother will be frightened of ghosts, so they can move back to America where they can go to a school for boys and girls, instead of the all-girl school they don't like. Mrs. Daniel suspects a poltergeist is causing the trouble, and her small son, Colin, thinks whatever a "poltergeist disease" is, he must have it. A story like this, with each character having a totally different approach to the plot of the story, can be handled skillfully in multiple viewpoint, enhancing the humor and suspense.

There is romance in this story—in this case the mother's romance with the man who rescues Colin, and the possible romance (that does not develop) with the former owner of the house. Romance is an important element in nearly every mystery novel for young adults, since it is of primary interest to most teen-agers. Sometimes it is a light, unimportant romance; sometimes it is essential to the plot. Usually, it involves the young adult characters themselves.

The Haunting of Ellen, by Catherine Sefton, is based on the story of a ghost named Margaret, who cannot rest until the real truth of the story of her flight with her lover, many years before, is known and explained. And in *Escape on Skis,* by Amelia Walden, it is Kim's love for her fiance that sends her to Switzerland to search for him, after he disappears without a word or sign.

Gothics

The Gothic mystery novel is a popular form of the young adult mystery, and here too romance is an integral part of the Gothic plot. The Gothic mystery is written to a formula: a young woman (usually in her late teens or early twenties) is alone and often in financial difficulties; she seeks help from relatives or friends of the family, or even applies for a job in a city where she knows no one. The people she goes to live with are strangers or people she doesn't know well. Perhaps they are distant relatives, estranged in the past by a family feud. In *The White Jade Fox,* by André Norton, Saranna Stowell goes to live with an uncle and cousin, after her father dies. She has never met them before, and the uncle sends her to a plantation home to act as governess for a young relative. Here she runs into mystery. which, in André Norton's hands, becomes a science fiction mystery.

Saranna's cousin is unkind to her, as is the housekeeper. She realizes there is a plot developing against her, a plot in which the handsome man next door—a man to whom she is very much attracted—may be involved.

In Sibyl Hancock's Gothic novel, *Mosshaven,* Heather O'Brien does not go to relatives for help when her father dies, but applies for a job in Galveston, Texas, because there are mysterious references to Galveston in her father's notes, and she wants to investigate them. She takes a job as companion to a wealthy woman. The romance in the story develops between Heather and one of the woman's two sons (the other one is also attracted to Heather); and the mystery revolves around the wealthy recluse, who seems to have a link to Heather's past.

Mosshaven and *The White Jade Fox* are historical Gothics, adding the interest of another period in time to the mystery and romance. However, Gothic mysteries can be contemporary in setting also. Phyllis A. Whitney's *Lost Island* is about Lacey, a modern woman, who flies to an island off the Georgia coast at the request of her cousin—a woman who, ten years before, stole the man Lacey loved, and even Lacey's son. While the plot in the contemporary Gothic takes place in the present, the mood of suspense and mystery, with the unhappy plight of the heroine and the misunderstanding between her and the man she is falling in love with (usually unwillingly), is common to both the historical and the contemporary Gothic novel.

There must be a great deal of action in the Gothic novel, and the background should be interesting and unusual. Quite often, the setting is a European country, or one of the more exotic spots in the United States. There is always a mood of disaster surrounding a Gothic; in fact, the story usually begins with this mood. Obligingly, the weather cooperates with thunderstorms and gray skies.

Although the heroine of the Gothic mystery is in a helpless, vulnerable situation—one from which she can't just walk away—she still must be a strong, independent character with a good share of intelligence, and the wits to be able to take care of herself in a dangerous situation. She should be feminine, yet not be a clinging vine, and there should be romantic scenes with the hero (avoiding explicit sex).

Mystery and history

The historical background can be used in other types of young adult mysteries besides the Gothic. Mary Stolz's *Cat in the Mirror* involves two girls: Erin, who lives in the present; and Irun, who lived in Egypt 3,000 years ago. Both have the same problem with their mothers, both have the same appearance, and both have a cat called Ta-she. It is during the second half of the novel, when the story is presented through Irun's eyes, that readers begin to realize that Erin and Irun are one and the same girl, living in different time periods. Besides the girls' problem, and the mystery, Mary Stolz gives readers a fascinating look at life in a wealthy home in ancient Egypt.

Writers who decide to set their mystery novels in any time period other than the present must do a thorough job of research, so that every detail in their novels will be accurate. In writing *Mosshaven,* Sibyl Hancock read every account she could find about the big hurricane of 1900 which nearly destroyed Galveston, so that she could use that storm in the climax of her novel. Aside from the books about the city of Galveston and the hurricane, she read old newspapers in scrapbook form, and newspaper accounts on microfilm in the library. She wrote the Galveston Historical Society, and one member took her on a tour of the city and told her many incidents and stories about life in Galveston in the 1900's, which were not recorded in books. She met people who had spent their lives in the city and were glad to show her through the historical homes in which they lived.

In addition to the facts about the city and the hurricane, the author had to know what kinds of clothing were being worn at this time, what foods people were serving at parties, what the social customs of the city were, what kinds of transportation were available, what kinds of business and trades were conducted there, how the women wore their hair, and so forth, down to the last detail.

The library is of great value to authors interested in writing historical fiction, because libraries have so many reference works. If the local library doesn't happen to have a certain volume for which an author is looking, it can often be borrowed from a library in another city through inter-library loans.

The Readers' Guide to Periodical Literature lists articles from over one hundred general magazines, and *Subject Guide to Books in Print* alphabetically arranges books by subject headings, so that everything in print is listed, with the author's name, title of the book, name of publisher, and year it was published.

Newspapers provide tremendous overall information about many periods, in their advertisements for clothes, recipes, and a variety of articles about events taking place at the time of publication. Furniture and fashion books often include drawings, photographs, and written descriptions of these items of past years.

Vocabulary should be consistent with the period in which the story takes place, so writers must take care not to use anachronisms—slang or other language not in use at the time.

As writers do their research, they can often get new ideas, or new twists to old ideas. Some of the material they unearth will take their plots in new, exciting directions. But they must be careful not to become so enamored of the material they have collected that they fill their mystery novels with facts, and let the story drag and the plot and pace suffer. Only a small part of the research collected should be included in the young adult historical mystery; but authors will have to know well the periods about which they write, so that they feel comfortable in their knowl-edge, and know they are writing with accuracy and authenticity.

The goals of the mystery novel for young adults are usually escapist entertainment and the creation of a main character with whom readers can identify, sharing the danger and excitement. However, occasionally the young adult mystery can deal with a current problem teenagers face, tying it in with the mystery, of course. *Call Me Al Raft,* by Richard Shaw, deals with a boy searching for his real father, trying to gain self-respect by finding out who his father was. And *Through a Brief Darkness,* by Richard Peck, tells the story through the viewpoint of a girl who discovers that her father is a member of a criminal syndicate.

In writing the young adult mystery, authors should stay away from trite subjects or mystery plots which have been overdone, and they should never "write down" to their readers. The problem should be taken seriously, on an adult level, and handled realistically. There can be dead bodies and more than one murder in young adult mysteries, but again, it's important not to include description that is too graphic. The story can be told in either first or third person—whichever seems to fit the story best.

Novels for the twelve-to-sixteen reader are longer than those for the eight-to-twelve age group. A mystery for young adults usually runs 30,000 to 40,000 words, with a maximum of around 60,000.

High interest—low reading level

A large number of junior high and high school students read on a level several grades below the grade they are in. Because of this, there are books published with special length and vocabulary requirements, but with high story interest, for these readers: Scholastic Action Books (for high school students reading on a second- to fourth-grade level), Albert Whitman and Company, and Franklin Watts, Inc., are examples of companies that publish high interest-low reading-level mystery novels.

The novels follow a certain pattern. Usually they are only 8,000 to 12,000 words long, with an average of 10,000 words, so that extra length won't frighten away reluctant or unskilled readers. Most of these books have ten chapters of about 1,000 words each. They contain a lot of action, short sentences, and words that can be read on an upper elementary reading level.

Stop, Thief! by William Butterworth, is a good example of how a story of this type opens with action and excitement. The arrangement of simple, not complex, sentences makes this book easier to read than the average young adult mystery:

> The police came for him just after his mother went to work.
> It was a little after eight in the morning. Paul had just come back from his night job at the garage. He was getting ready for bed. Then he heard a loud knock at the door.
> "Just a minute," Paul called. He went to the door and opened it a little. But he left the chain on.
> There were two policemen in the hall.
> "Paul Sears?" one of them asked.
> "Yes," Paul said.
> "Open the door. We want to talk to you."

Paul is accused of being an accomplice in a car theft from the garage in which he works. Because one of the police officers believes in him, Paul works out a plan to catch the real car thieves.

Norma Ruedi Ainsworth's *Mystery of the Crying Child* deals with a contemporary problem to which many girls can relate. As the story opens, Jane is shown wanting to prove herself at a janitorial job that has traditionally been given to boys. Because of her job she is led into the mystery, and the mystery complicates her problem of holding the job and proving she can do it:

> "A girl can do any job a boy can," Jane had said.
> "But this is no work for a girl. This is dirty work," Uncle Bill had told her.

Jane had laughed at him. "Uncle Bill, you are old-fashioned. I can do the job. I need the money. And I am just as strong as Jim. Look!" She had picked up a chair and held it over her head with one hand.

So Uncle Bill had given in. "OK, the job is yours. We will see how you work out."

That was two weeks ago. Now Jane was racing up to the fourth floor of Number 13 to pick up the trash . . .

Readers of the young adult mystery developed their love of mysteries during their elementary school years and are ready-made mystery fans who will carry that reading interest through their adult lives. It is exciting to authors of teenage mysteries to know that there is a group of eager readers waiting to welcome each new young adult mystery as it is released by the publishers.

11

Magazine Mysteries

BECAUSE mystery stories are so popular with young readers, they are found in many magazines for children, regardless of the type of magazine or the age group for which it is aimed. Whether it's *Sprint,* Scholastic's school-related publication for 9- to 11-year-olds who read at 4th to 6th grade levels, *The Friend,* a denominational paper for the youngest children, or *'Teen,* aimed at high school girls, the editors are looking for good, short mystery stories for their readers.

The basic rules for writing mystery novels also apply to writing short mystery fiction for magazines: an interesting main character presented in the opening of the story; a problem this character must solve; lots of well-paced dialogue; appeal to the reader's senses; strong action verbs. Also, enough description should be used to give a clear picture of what the author wants the reader to see, but because of the limited number of words the writer may use for the short mystery story, descriptions of people and places should be kept to a minimum, with description of the action receiving the most emphasis and space.

The single viewpoint is essential in the magazine-length

story, even in the mystery for the young adult reader. There simply isn't enough space in a short story to get deeply into the viewpoints of various characters, and jumping back and forth between the minds of two or more characters gives the story an erratic, hopscotch effect, eliminating any chance for reader identification.

Because of the limited length of a magazine mystery, the mystery must be kept simple. There is usually just one facet to the short mystery, no detailed, complicated interaction that would need explanation at the end of the story. The number of characters is kept to a minimum, too. Whereas in a story of novel length an entire family can be involved, along with assorted other characters who people the mystery, in the magazine-length mystery story, there will probably be only two or three characters in addition to the main character.

"High Rise Mystery," by Catherine Campbell (*Jack and Jill*), has to do with Tina, who has a morning job delivering newspapers to the people in her apartment house. She wants to earn enough money to buy a bicycle. Her boss, Mr. Smith, informs her that one of the customers has not been getting her paper, and Tina has to find out why, since she's been faithfully delivering it. Tina hides in the stairway to watch, but wanting to get to school on time makes her leave before the culprit arrives. The next day she tries again and discovers the thief is Danny, the boy who lost the job because he wasn't dependable. He is reacting in desperation, because his father is out of work. Tina goes to Mr. Smith with the problem, and he suggests the two of them share the paper route. In the solution of the problem, Tina knows she'll get her bike after all, and she is willing to help Danny, even though it will take longer to reach her goal.

The plot is simple, the mystery one that can be solved without complication, the personal problem is intertwined with the mystery, and the number of characters in the story is only three. Even though the solution to the problem is suggested to Tina, it is still up to her to do it and to accept the consequences. Her willingness to help Danny provides the real solution to the personal problem in the mystery.

Techniques

The opening in a magazine-length mystery should contain a great deal of information in relatively few words, and make the reader want to read on—to finish the story. Dorothy Van Woerkom's "The Secret of the Oak Tree" (*Young Miss*) brings in the main character, the setting, and the hint of mystery in the first paragraph:

> Over the trim shoulders of David, her grandmother's chauffeur, Jenifer Cardin watched the Mississippi River sweep beneath the long high bridge; for no reason she could name her stomach did a flip-flop. Behind the slow-moving traffic, New Orleans backed up onto the levee like a giant crawfish. Ahead lay the mysterious Louisiana Bayou country—an exciting place for a Philadelphia girl to spend her fourteenth summer. Jenifer smiled. What would Mom and Dad say when they learned that she had flown straight into the middle of a mystery and, if her luck held, a hurricane?

Action verbs give strength to the mystery story as well as eliminating the need for longer passages of description. This passage from "The Secret of the Oak Tree" shows the power of action verbs in this paragraph, as Jenifer tries to make her way to the pirogue to get help:

> She crouched against the rain, slipping and sliding on the wet clay, clutching at the graves to keep from falling. The bayou had risen and was washing up over the lower graves.

Suspense must be developed quickly in the story.

Although the title will undoubtedly inform readers that this story is going to be a mystery, they ought to become involved in the action and suspense of the story as close to the beginning of the story as possible. Suspense is tied in with curiosity, and the curious child must read on to see what will happen next!

Quite often in the magazine mystery, the main character gets involved in the mystery because of her own sense of curiosity. Jenifer wants to know why her grandmother is getting threatening letters; and in "The Treasure Map," by Iva Nell Elder (*Guide for Juniors*), Jim is obsessed by his curiosity when he finds a buried treasure map in his backyard, decodes the mirror writing, and tries to find the treasure.

In Jim's case, the mystery story has a moral to it, as do many of the stories in religious magazines. Jim's treasure map turns out to be a trick played on him by his father, who is attempting to show his son why his friends don't like it when Jim constantly plays tricks on them.

Normally, writers try hard to disguise any messages or morals within their stories, but some religious magazines— not all of them—require the moral to be evident, even in a mystery. The only way in which writers can know an editor's preference in this regard is to become familiar with the magazines for which they want to write.

Knowing a magazine and having an awareness of the age group for which it is published are essentials for writers who want to sell their stories. Age levels determine both the subject of the story and its length. Prospective mystery writers often fall short on one of these points. I have seen manuscripts in which the content was suitable for five- or six-year-old readers, but the lengths were 3,000 or even 6,000 words! If the writers had checked the requirements of the magazines for these age groups, they'd see that *Highlights for Children,* for example, wants stories of 400 to 600 words—or occasionally 1,000 words. *Jack and Jill* likes 500 to 1,200 words; and *Story Friends* wants only 350 to 900 words. Familiarity with the magazines would help writers plan story lengths in advance so they would not be faced with the discouraging task of cutting a 3,000-word manuscript down to 600 words.

Although writers need to know the specific requirements of any magazine to which they want to submit stories, there are suggested lengths for various age groups. For the primary grade age group, the best length is 300 to 500 words, with an absolute maximum of 900 words. For the elementary and junior-high ages, where the story usually appeals to both boys and girls and the plot is more exciting, the length can be anywhere from 1,000 to 2,000 words, but 1,500 seems to be the most popular length.

In mystery stories for teen-agers, there is more of a division by type. Girls' stories must have a romance of some sort, even if it's just a hint of a romance; boys' stories tend toward having more adventure. The best length here is under 2,000 words, but stories can run as long as 3,000 words for some teen-age magazines.

Magazines reflect individual editorial style and taste. By studying magazines, writers can see that some of them prefer character-oriented mysteries; others like stronger plots; some appeal more to girls than to boys (or vice versa); and some require a denominational slant. Writers should send for fact sheets from the magazines for which they want to write, but there is still no substitute for careful reading of the magazines and knowing fairly well the type of story for which a particular editor is looking. Magazines not sold on the stands—primarily religious magazines—can be purchased directly from their publishing companies, sometimes for just the cost of postage. Editors of these magazines are eager to find good writers—particularly writers who are willing to take the time to study their magazines and send what they think will best meet editorial requirements. Lists of juvenile magazines, with their addresses, names of editors, and editorial requirements, including word length and type of story wanted, may be found in such volumes as *The Writer's Handbook, The Writer,* and *Literary Market Place.*

Plotting the 300-word story

The idea of writing a story in only 300 words or so can be a frightening one to a prospective writer. How could anyone get a plot, characterization, setting, and all the rest into a story of only that length? It's a challenge, to be sure, but it can be done. In a picture book, where many stories are close to that length, the story is carried partially by the illustrations; in the magazine mystery story of that length, there are often only one or two illustrations, and the story is on its own.

The story of just a few hundred words is obviously for the very young child, and that child's world is quite small. A mystery for that age group would be a "puzzle" mystery—something that would not frighten the child—with an uncomplicated plot.

Just how can a writer work out a complete story in only 300 words? One approach would be to break down the plot of the story into one sentence. Suppose it's an idea about a howling dog—a dog that is making a strange, crying noise. Maybe the idea could involve a mystery as to exactly what is making this weird noise, a puzzle, until the child realizes the sound is coming from a dog. Then the plot would involve the child's investigating to find out why the dog is crying like that, and the solution in which the child does something to help the dog. So, summed up in one sentence, it could read something like this: Johnny, frightened by a strange, howling noise, becomes courageous enough to investigate, discovers that a crying dog has trapped itself inside an old packing box, and sets the dog free. From that basic sentence, the story could be written.

Naturally, there wouldn't be any spare words to describe Johnny and his surroundings in detail. Some of this could be conveyed in the illustration that would accompany the magazine story. The writer has to get directly into the action, probably by beginning the story with the frightening sound of the dog's crying and its effect on Johnny. By being careful of excess wordage and using no characters other than Johnny and the dog, a writer could keep this story well inside the 300-word limit.

This same story idea could be developed into a longer, more involved magazine story for older children by making Johnny older, adding a friend for him, and perhaps an adult character or two. In this case, a colorful or mysterious setting could be used. Maybe the howling or crying has been heard before, but nothing has been found when an attempt was made to track it down. The longer story for older children could involve a missing poodle and an old woman who tearfully asks Johnny and his friend to look for her dog. She might mention someone else whose dog disappeared a few weeks before. Johnny and his friend begin to add things up. Could this be a case of dognapping? How are they to find the dognappers? Perhaps they could set a trap.

In the very short story, the writer must cut out every excess word and also any nonessential characters, superfluous descriptions or plot complications and any complexity of the mystery itself that is not absolutely required. In the shorter story about Johnny and the dog, for example, there is no villain, no criminal element; it is just a puzzle for the main character. He has to find out what is making the frightening sound and do something about it.

Cutting and tightening

Writers can pare unnecessary length from their stories for all age groups in a number of ways. Aside from making a story fit magazine length requirements, this pruning can result in a tighter, faster-paced story.

Unnecessary words can be eliminated. Too often, a sentence can become wordy—especially in writing dialogue, when a writer tries to make it sound natural by including too much. For example, here are two ways that dialogue can be written:

> "Hey, wait a minute," Harry said. He scuffed the toe of one shoe back and forth in the dust on the road, and looked toward the old house. "Are you sure you want us to go inside? I mean, there's really no reason why we should all go inside, is there? Wouldn't it work out better if one of us—maybe me—stayed outside to be a look-out?"
>
> Bob stared at him for a full minute before he answered. "It sounds to me like you're scared to go inside the house," he said.
>
> "Well," Harry said. "Well, if you put it that way—maybe I am!"

And the other way, by cutting and tightening:

> "Wait a minute!" Harry said. He looked toward the old house. "We don't all need to go inside, do we? Why don't I stay outside and be a look-out?"
>
> Bob stared at him. "I think you're scared to go inside the house."
>
> "Well," Harry said. "Maybe I am!"

Descriptive passages can be cut. This is sometimes hard on writers, because they feel that descriptive writing is often their best writing; but when it comes to tightening a story, it's usually the description that has to go. In this paragraph the location could be described in detail:

> Jed stood on the sand and examined the cliffs again. The rough and craggy surface of the weathered rocks that had been fashioned by centuries of pounding waves was softened now in the late afternoon shadows. Rivulets of water trickled from the lower ledges, where the tide had been not long ago, and barnacles clung tenaciously in a shiny blue-black pattern. Jed

climbed over the nearest boulder and found himself in a small cove. There, in the side of the cliff, was the cave for which they had all been searching.

However, with much of the needless description cut out, the paragraph gives the essentials and the story moves along:

It was late afternoon, and the tide was out when Jed explored the beach again. He found himself in a small cove, and there, in the side of the cliff, was the cave for which they had all been searching.

Occasionally, mystery fiction writers find it necessary to explain to a character in the story the discovery of a clue or an occurrence which the readers have already seen taking place. Instead of repeating the scene in the story, it can be handled as Catherine Campbell did in her "High Rise Mystery":

The next morning Tina told Mr. Smith what had happened. ". . . and Danny's sore because I have his job when his family needs the money."

Sometimes an entire scene can be cut out of a story, and the information in it capsulized or condensed in a short transitional sentence or paragraph. Sometimes, an unnecessary character can be omitted altogether, if he or she is not important to the action of the story, and leaving him out won't make any difference to the plot or story line.

Serials

A magazine may give a writer even greater leeway in the matter of length for a serial of two or more parts. For a two-part serial, *Jack and Jill* sets lengths of 1,200 words per installment. *Jet Cadet,* on the other hand, wants 1,000-word installments for a two-part serial, for a total of 2,000 words.

Many editors are looking for these two-part serials or want to see queries and outlines for them. The stories must be carefully divided into the proper number of installments, so that in a two-part serial there is a real "cliff-hanger" at the end of the first part, and readers will pick up the magazine eagerly, to read what comes in the next installment.

The author can write a short synopsis of the first installment, which can be used at the beginning of the second part. This synopsis will summarize in one short paragraph what has happened in the first part. It should also seem exciting to readers who have not read the first installment but will want to read the second. Editors can and often do write these synopses of the previously published sections, but there is no reason the authors can't do so.

Here is an example of a good synopsis (from *Teen Magazine*) of Part I of Audrey Lazier's serial, "The Case of the Purloined Ghost," which precedes the second part:

> *Synopsis of Part I.* Strange things have been happening at the summer theatre where Tish is working. Props are missing, lights have gone out mysteriously during performances. No one can solve the mystery. Tish would rather pay attention to Greg, who is playing Hamlet's father's ghost, but the dilemma at hand must be dealt with—immediately!

There are many juvenile magazines being published today, most of them with an "open door" policy toward new writers—especially those who can come up with exciting, well-written mysteries that will interest young readers.

12

Marketing the Juvenile Mystery

AT LAST, the juvenile mystery book or short story manuscript is finished and ready for market. The writer is eager to submit the work to juvenile book publishing companies or children's magazines, hoping to find acceptance for publication.

What are the important steps to take now? First of all, the manuscript must be professionally presented, with careful attention to appearance and readability.

In preparing a juvenile mystery manuscript for submission, be sure you type it double space, on a good grade of typing paper. There should be a title page with the author's name and address in the upper left-hand corner, and the approximate number of words in the upper right-hand corner. In the center of the page, the title is typed in capital letters, with "by" under it, and the author's name under that. The first page of the manuscript should look exactly like the title page, except that the story begins on the lower part of the page—halfway or two-thirds of the way down.

On each following page, the author's name or the title of

the story should be typed in the left-hand corner, to identify each page if the pages are accidentally separated in the
publishing office. In the right-hand corner, type the page
number, beginning with page 2.

The author should always keep a carbon copy of the
manuscript. When submitting the manuscript, always enclose a self-addressed envelope with sufficient postage for
the return of the manuscript. A short story of five or six
pages can be folded into thirds and sent in a #10 envelope.
The stamped return envelope, of the same size, should be
folded in thirds and enclosed. A manuscript of more than
five or six pages should be sent flat in a 9" x 12" manila
envelope, with a stamped, self-addressed envelope of the
same size folded in half and enclosed. A book-length manuscript may be mailed in a padded book-mailer or a box (the
kind typing paper comes in).

If the author has had any previous contact or encouragement from the editor to whom the manuscript is going, it's
a good idea to enclose a cover letter, mentioning the earlier
comment. Cover letters should be short, and the reasons for
sending one with a manuscript should be clear. It is useless
to write a cover letter saying, "Here is my manuscript. I
hope you like it." However, if an author has received a
friendly letter of rejection on a previous manuscript, and
the editor has suggested that he or she would like to see
anything else the writer would care to submit, he can refer
to the editor's letter. This is likely to take a manuscript past
the first reader and reach the editor who wrote the author
originally.

Only one copy of the manuscript should be in circula-
tion—the original. It's not a good idea to submit a repro-
duced copy of a manuscript, since the editor may assume
from receiving a duplicated copy of a manuscript that the
same novel or story was submitted simultaneously to a
number of publishers. It's hard for impatient authors to

send out manuscripts and wait for months to have their manuscripts evaluated by editors who return them with perhaps a simple, printed form rejection. Then the manuscripts must be sent out again, with possibly another long wait before rejection, or—one always hopes—acceptance. Unfortunately, no one has been able to come up with an answer to this problem. Editors want to feel that they have an exclusive right to consider a book manuscript to see if it would fit into their overall publishing plans, what possibilities it would have for subsidiary rights sales, what the marketing department thinks about the manuscript's subsidiary rights sales, and what the marketing department thinks about the manuscript's sales potential. Several editors in a juvenile department may want to read and discuss the manuscript, and in some cases, editors will ask outside readers—teachers or librarians—to read the manuscript and offer their opinions. If a manuscript is being offered at the same time to a number of publishing houses, many editors would rather not consider the manuscript. While we occasionally hear of the agent of a famous author offering an adult "blockbuster novel" for bids, this sales technique hasn't reached into the children's book departments yet.

Some publishing houses, in order to cut expenses, have closed their doors to open submission of manuscripts, asking authors to write describing the manuscript they wish to send, and to submit it only if they get a go-ahead from an editor.

How long should writers wait for replies about their manuscripts? Editors often run into extra-busy periods and find it hard to reply as soon as they would like to. Patience is a key word among writers, and the patient writer, who doesn't rush to ask the editor the status of his manuscript after two or three weeks have gone by, is more likely to sell his stories.

However, if a story manuscript has been sent to a maga-

zine and no communication from the editor has been received after six to eight weeks, it's a good idea to write and
ask the editor about it. For a book-length manuscript, the
writer may reasonably expect to have some response in two
to three months. After that, the writer may send a letter to
inquire. Perhaps it was lost in the mail and the editor hasn't
received it. Send a short, courteous letter, telling when the
manuscript was mailed and its title, and ask about its current status. The writer's name and address should be on the
letter and the envelope.

Since writers are creative people, they don't usually like
the mundane tasks concerning the business side of writing.
Yet it's essential to keep an accurate record of where manuscripts are sent, the dates on which they were mailed, and
the dates returned—or sold.

Revisions and rewrites

It's always a thrill for an author, no matter how many
books he or she may have had published, to receive a letter
from an editor saying a manuscript has been accepted
for publication. But in almost every case, along with the
acceptance come editorial suggestions for revision, which
can vary from the changing of a confusing word in a sentence to ideas for rewriting an entire chapter, or even reor-
ganizing and reworking much of the book.

It can be distressing for authors to have editors ask
them to cut some of their favorite passages, or make major
changes in their manuscripts; yet the job of editors is to
edit. Capable editors know the market, have a fairly good
idea of the kind of books that are being bought and why,
have a critical eye for sentences that are awkward or too
long, for characters that need to be more fully developed,
for story lines that bog down in places, and for all the other
errors over which authors may trip. Editors will not usually
make major changes in authors' manuscripts; they will sug-

gest the changes they think necessary and ask the writers to do the revisions. If a change is disturbing to an author, then it may be discussed, and an agreement reached that satisfies both author and editor; but in most cases it's better for the author to trust the editor's judgment and get to work immediately on the manuscript, making the suggested changes with a professional attitude.

Rejections

The types of rejection slips or letters a writer receives can be confusing. A form rejection letter is exactly that: Editors receive thousands of manuscripts each year, and they must reject most of them. A form letter, whether printed or typed, means the editor is offering no encouragement to the writer to revise the manuscript.

Sometimes at the bottom of a form letter, an editor or publisher will write or type a short message to the author. It may be a simple "sorry," or even a "try us again." This is intended to offer some encouragement, and the author who receives such a note should definitely submit another manuscript to that editor. The short note simply indicates that the editor found some merit in the manuscript. While writers would like a detailed critique on each manuscript rejected, it would be impossible for editors, who often must read manuscripts in their spare moments at home, to find time to write critiques.

Occasionally, an author gets a personal letter from the editor with a rejected manuscript. This is the best kind of encouragement. The editor is letting the author know that although this manuscript will not be purchased, his work has been carefully considered and is appreciated. Whatever editors say, they mean. If a letter says, "We would like to see any other manuscript you would care to submit," the editor means it. If it says, "Please try us again in six months, if you haven't sold this manuscript by then," be

sure you do so. One of my students who received a letter
like that said, "I thought she was just being polite, and I
threw the letter away and forgot about it!"

Editorial requirements and trends

Authors wish there were some magic way in which they
could know exactly what kind of manuscript a particular
editor is looking for. Editors themselves don't always
know or they don't want to pinpoint their needs, knowing
that a special manuscript could come in that would delight
them and be totally unlike any of their preconceived ideas
or stated requirements of what they "need." An editor
will want to buy a juvenile mystery if her house is publishing mysteries, if it fits the right age group, and if it's
exciting, fun to read, and will offer the reader an extra value
in understanding a common problem, or learning about a
new land, culture or profession. There is a great interest
now in occult mystery novels—the unexplained ghost, the
poltergeist, the warlock or witch, and evil preternatural
forces. Settings in England, Scotland and Wales, particularly
along the coasts, seem to be favorite backgrounds for juvenile mysteries.

Authors can find out about editors' requirements by
making a thorough study of the current market news and
listings of juvenile magazines and book publishers (with
their addresses, names of editors, and basic information
about their specific needs) in the writers' magazines, *The
Writer's Handbook,* and *Literary Market Place.* By studying
publishers' catalogues, authors can see what kinds of books
are on the new lists. Most publishers are glad to send these
catalogues to authors at no cost.

To make current marketing information easier for me to
find, I keep a card file of facts about children's book publishers, which includes the names of editors and assistant
editors, preferred age groups for which their books are pub-

lished, and other bits of information I run across.

It's important for authors of juvenile mysteries to keep up with what is being published in this field. The best help is to read as many of the current juvenile mysteries as possible. Library browsing is very useful for this purpose. By leafing through the new books, authors can find which publishers seem to prefer action-adventure mysteries, and which like the occult mystery; which include light romance with the mysteries in their published books, and which completely omit the romantic angle; which favor British settings—fogs, moors, and cliffside villages; and which publish mystery novels where characterization in depth is as important as the mystery plot itself.

Since very few libraries can afford to buy every juvenile mystery published, writers can supplement their knowledge by reading reviews of these books. The largest number of reviews of juvenile books can be found in *School Library Journal, The Horn Book, Publishers Weekly, Booklist,* and *The New York Times Book Review* in their special children's book editions each spring and fall. Other magazines review children's books in every issue, and most large newspapers (like *The Christian Science Monitor, Los Angeles Times, Book World, West Coast Review of Books,* etc.) and magazines will carry reviews of children's books from time to time.

Subsidiary rights, extra benefits

There are many opportunities for subsidiary rights in the field of the juvenile mystery novel. Some publishers have active subsidiary rights departments that submit galleys of a book or the finished book to book clubs, paperback reprint publishers, and publishers in other countries. Most book club selections are made from such submissions by the publishers' subsidiary rights department, but authors can request the subsidiary rights department to send copies of their books to a specific place, such as a foreign publisher, if they know there is a demand for the book abroad.

Juvenile mysteries can bring authors extra benefits in a number of ways. An excerpt from one of my mystery novels is used in a nation-wide school reading program, and an adaptation of *Secret Box Mystery* is included in a textbook. Books for younger children, especially, are sometimes purchased for reprinting in textbooks. Juvenile book authors have had their books adapted for radio shows, television programs, and puppet shows; and their books have been sold to publishers in other countries to be printed in various languages. Juvenile books have been serialized and/or condensed in magazines and newspapers, and even made into full-length feature movies.

Agents

Although literary agents can be helpful in many ways, such as obtaining some subsidiary rights which authors might not think of trying by themselves, and working out contracts that might be more beneficial to authors, it is not essential for an author in the juvenile field to have an agent. In fact, most reputable agents will not take on as a client a writer who has not sold extensively. Although many beginning writers think an agent is an immediate passport to success, the agent can't sell a story on the strength of his or her name alone. The story or novel has to be publishable to be accepted, whether it comes in through an agent or not. Some editors do feel that agents, who have given manuscripts a pre-reading, will send only what they think the editors will like; and in this way, the agented manuscript might get a faster reading or have a slight advantage. In the final reading, however, at most publishing houses, the manuscript that delights the editor will be accepted for publication even if it has come in the "slush pile" or "over the transom"—designations for unsolicited manuscripts. And every manuscript is read, so that even beginning writers have a good chance of finding a home for their manuscripts.

A list of agents who belong to the Society of Author's Representatives can be found in *The Writer's Handbook* and *Literary Market Place.*

Professional writers associations

Many authors find it beneficial to belong to a national writers' group; and there are two which serve the needs of authors of juvenile mysteries.

One is the Mystery Writers of America, Inc., 105 East 19th Street, New York, N.Y. 10003. It is an organization of mystery writers in all fields: magazine, novel, television, short story, screenplay, and juvenile mystery; and it consistently works to improve the lot of mystery writers and their prestige in the field of writing.

Each April, the Mystery Writers of America present the Edgar Allan Poe awards for the best mystery writing in each mystery category, small busts of Poe called "Edgars." Runners-up are presented with Special Scroll awards. Occasionally, special awards are given—statues of Poe's "Raven."

There are five chapters of the MWA in the United States: New York, New England, Midwest, Northern California and Southern California; and there is an at-large membership for those living in the United States, but not conveniently near one of the chapters.

There are four classifications of membership in MWA: *Active,* for anyone who has made at least one sale in the field of mystery, suspense or crime writing (fact or fiction). Only active members may hold office or vote. *Associate,* for non-writers who are allied to the mystery field—editors, publishers, critics, literary agents, motion picture, radio, or television producers. *Corresponding membership,* for writers living outside the United States, whether they are American citizens or not. *Affiliate,* for new writers who have not yet made a sale, or for non-writers who are mystery enthusiasts.

All members are sent copies of the newsletter, "The Third Degree," published every other month; and each April they receive the Mystery Writers' Annual, in magazine format, which is published in conjunction with the annual MWA Edgar awards, "The Third Degree" frequently includes market information for mystery writers.

Another national writers' group, made up of writers for children, is the Society of Children's Book Writers, P.O. Box 296, Los Angeles, California 90006. This organization is open to authors, editors, publishers, illustrators, librarians, educators and agents who are interested in children's literature. SCBW offers full membership to anyone who has had at least one children's book or story published within the last six years. Associate memberships are open to anyone who is interested in children's literature, published or not.

Each year, SCBW holds a writers' conference in the Los Angeles area and sponsors regional conferences in Massachusetts, Houston, and other areas. At the Los Angeles conference, the Golden Kite awards for best children's books by members are announced. Members receive a bi-monthly bulletin, which tells what members are doing in the field of publishing, includes market news from publishers of juvenile books, answers authors' questions pertaining to writing and publishing, and shares ideas from active members.

Most cities have local writers' clubs, and these can be of benefit to writers who want the stimulation of ideas and encouragement from other writers. Some clubs have meetings at which manuscripts are read aloud and critiqued, some have guest speakers from the publishing and writing field, and some utilize the talents of the members to provide programs of instruction in various forms of writing. If a city does not have a writers' club, and a writer wants to join one, it's usually easy to organize one. If there are even three or four writers who share an interest in having such an organization, they can begin with a small group, and a little publicity will bring them other members. They might consider forming a writers' group as a study group adjunct to another, larger organization like the American Association of University Women, or the YWCA. And if a local college or university has a writing course, they can ask to recruit members from the students in the class. The world is full of writers and people interested in writing. It's a lonely profession, and writers are often eager to meet with other writers who understand what the process is all about.

Throughout the year, especially during the spring and summer months, writers' conferences are held in many places in the United States. These are open to professional and beginning writers, and are usually quite helpful to both. The various workshops offer instruction, new ideas and information; provide writers with the chance to talk to the editors in attendance, who can give writers a clearer picture of the current trends and requirements in publishing; and offer unlimited opportunities for shop-talk with other writers who are there to share ideas which can be informative and encouraging.

Some conferences are a week to two weeks long, and offer a regular period of class instruction, in addition to the side benefits of meeting the visiting authors, editors, and literary agents. Most conferences are of shorter duration—two or three days packed full of lectures, workshops, and discussions. Either type of conference sends the writer off with a sense of direction in his writing, a head full of exciting ideas, and an eagerness to get to the typewriter—which is the main purpose of any writers' conference.

Using the discipline to stick to a schedule at the typewriter, applying the rules of the writing craft, and making use of the techniques of the juvenile mystery field, a writer can be well on the way to becoming a published author of juvenile mysteries.